Elena Jotow   Nicholas Ganz

Burma
THE ALTERNATIVE GUIDE

မြန်မာပြည် ခရီးသွားလမ်းညွှန် အခြားနည်းလမ်း

with 243 illustrations and 8 colour maps

Thames & Hudson

For the people of Burma   မြန်မာပြည်သူပြည်သားများအတွက်

Translated from German by David H. Wilson

First published in the United Kingdom in 2009
by Thames & Hudson Ltd, 181A High Holborn,
London WC1V 7QX

www.thamesandhudson.com

© 2009 Elena Jotow and Nicholas Ganz

British Library Cataloguing-in-Publication Data
A catalogue record for this book is available from
the British Library

ISBN 978-0-500-28787-3

Printed and bound in China by
C&C Offset Printing Co. Ltd

On the cover
(front, from top to bottom) *pathein
hti* umbrellas, Bassein, Irrawaddy
Division; protesting monk, Saffron
Revolution, Rangoon; Myohaung
at dawn, Arakan State
(back, clockwise from top left)
Light Festival, Shwedagon Pagoda,
Rangoon; Buddha statues at the foot
of Mount Zwekabin, Karen State;
Buddhist monk, Shwedagon Pagoda;
Intha man, Lake Inle, Shan State

Page 1: rural landscape near
Myohaung
Preceding pages: pagoda near
Bhamo, Kachin State
Below: Kaladan riverbank, Arakan
State

Picture Credits
p. 140 Karl Förster; p. 141 Free
Burma Rangers; p. 144 (bottom left)
Burma Digest; p. 162 Burma Issues;
p. 172 Alain Evrard (Impact Photos);
p. 177 Moustache Brothers; pp. 178
(top) & 180 Mizzima News; p. 178
(bottom) Yair Pike; p. 195 Back Pack
Health Worker Team. All other
photographs by Nicholas Ganz.

Contents မာတိကာ

Preface နိဒါန်း

Burma is known as the land of the golden pagodas, with an ancient culture and a religious tradition that have persisted right through to the present day. It is a country of many different races and creeds, though little is known about some of the minority groups. Thanks to the predominance of Buddhism, the tourist will find himself choosing between thousands of temples and shrines, but beneath this shining, tranquil surface lies a history of bitter conflict. This book describes the Burma we got to know during the course of our travels. Our account covers the richness of the culture and the friendliness of the people, who welcomed us wherever we went, but also the tragic tales recounted to us by refugees.

Visitors require permission from the tourism authorities to enter various parts of the country, and there are some towns and regions (such as Chin State and Karenni State) that foreigners are simply not allowed to enter. Other than passport holders from ASEAN countries, China, Bangladesh and Russia, all foreign visitors need to apply for a visa to enter Burma. A tourist visa is valid for ninety days after issue and allows a visit of twenty-eight days. Travellers' cheques and credit cards are rarely accepted in Burma, and tourists usually have to pay for accommodation and travel in US dollars, which invariably goes straight to the military.

These restrictions and limitations made it impossible for us to cover the whole country. However, we have tried to give a comprehensive and objective insight into the complex realities of this South-East Asian land, in all its beauty and in all its harshness, for the two are inextricably linked and make their indelible mark on the country and its people. After the extraordinary events of September 2007, it may be that Burma is gradually entering a process of political change. What had long seemed completely impossible suddenly became real for just a few weeks: the power and determination of the people made them rise up against their oppressors, and even though the military were able eventually to crush the demonstrators, they could not crush the nation's desire for freedom and democracy.

We have used the traditional English names of towns and regions, but for the sake of clearer orientation have sometimes added in parentheses the new names given to them by the military junta in 1989.

We hope with this book to provide an informative introduction to the rich but troubled culture and people of this endlessly fascinating country.

**Buddhist monk,
Shwedagon Pagoda,
Rangoon**

Elena Jotow and Nicholas Ganz, Autumn 2008

Burma at a Glance

မြန်မာပြည်အကြောင်းတစေ့တစောင်း

With an area of 676,577 square kilometres (261,228 mi^2), Burma is the largest country on the South-East Asian peninsula – almost three times the size of Great Britain. It measures 2,050 kilometres (1,274 mi) in length, and at its broadest point from east to west it is 935 kilometres (581 mi) wide. In the north and east it borders on China, Laos and Thailand, and in the west on Bangladesh and India, while the southern coast lies on the Bay of Bengal and the Andaman Sea.

Since 1962, the country has been ruled by a military dictatorship, and in the regions along the eastern border there is still a vicious civil war in progress. Estimates of the population vary between 50 and 55 million, but there has never been a reliable census; the last count took place back in 1983, and only in the areas under military control. Until November 2005, the capital was Rangoon (Yangon), with a population of around 5 million. However, the seat of government was then moved to Naypyidaw, about 200 kilometres (124 mi) north of Rangoon. The second-largest city is Mandalay (approximately 1 million people).

With 135 officially recognized ethnic groups, Burma is a multiracial state in which over 100 languages and dialects are spoken. The majority of the people, about 70%, are said to be Burmese (also called Bamar or Burman), and they are the dominant force politically, economically and culturally. Other ethnic groups dispute these figures, claiming that 50% would be closer to the mark, and accuse the government of massaging the statistics in favour of the Burmese. The largest non-Burmese ethnic peoples are the Shan (8.5%), the Karen (6.2%), the Arakanese (4.5%), the Mon (2.4%), the Chin (2.2%) and the Kachin (1.4%), most of whom live in the border regions. Between 1% and 2% of the population are said to be Indian and Chinese immigrants.

The principal language is Burmese, which belongs to the Tibeto-Burmese language family, as do Arakanese, Chin, Kachin, Akha, Lisu, Lahu and Naga. The Mon, Wa and Palaung speak Mon-Khmer languages, while the Shan belong to the Tai group. The languages of the Karen (also known as Kayin), Karenni (Kayah) and Pa-O are independent of all these groups.

The religious majority, with 89%, are followers of Theravada Buddhism, but some 4% of the population practise Islam and another 4% Christianity, and among the ethnic minorities an important role is played by animism, which is also reflected in everyday life throughout Burma. Nearly every

Burma has fourteen administrative states and divisions, which are numbered on this map as follows:
 1 Rangoon Division
 2 Irrawaddy Division
 3 Arakan State
 4 Magwe Division
 5 Chin State
 6 Sagaing Division
 7 Kachin State
 8 Shan State
 9 Mandalay Division
10 Karenni State
11 Pegu Division
12 Karen State
13 Mon State
14 Tenasserim
    Division

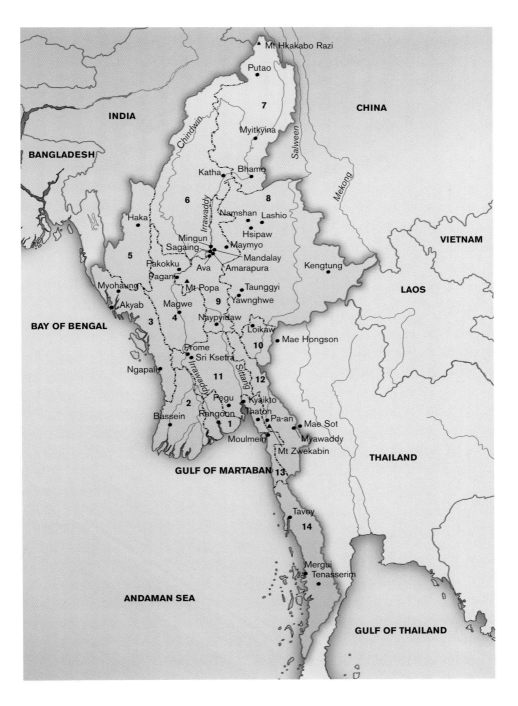

Mt Hkakabo Razi

Putao

INDIA

CHINA

7

Chindwin

Myitkyina

Salween

BANGLADESH

Katha   Bhamo

Mekong

6

Irrawaddy

8

Haka

Namshan   Lashio

5

Hsipaw

Mingun   Maymyo
Sagaing

VIETNAM

Pakokku   Mandalay
Pagan   Ava   Amarapura

Kengtung

LAOS

Myohaung

Mt Popa   Taunggyi

Akyab   Magwe   9   Yawnghwe

BAY OF BENGAL

3   4   Naypyidaw

Loikaw

10   Mae Hongson

Prome
Sri Ksetra

Ngapali

Irrawaddy

11   Sittang   12

2   Pegu   Kyaikto
Bassein   Rangoon   Thaton   Pa-an   Mae Sot
1   Myawaddy

Moulmein

Mt Zwekabin   THAILAND

GULF OF MARTABAN 13

Tavoy

14

Mergui
Tenasserim

ANDAMAN SEA

GULF OF THAILAND

household has a little altar at which sacrifices are made to different *nats* (spirits), to ask for protection and good fortune.

Since 1987, Burma has been classified by the United Nations as a *least developed country* (LDC), which is based on the criteria of low income, weak human resources and economic vulnerability. Its infrastructure and industry are for the most part badly underdeveloped, and 75% of the people live on agriculture. Poverty is widespread, with many barely scraping a living from the land, while wages are generally very low – a doctor's or teacher's average wage is around £3.50 ($7) a month. Life expectancy is 60.5 years, but nearly half the population are under the age of twenty.

Thanks to the catastrophic policies of the military dictatorship, the health system is in an appalling state. Only 3% of the national budget is devoted to it, while almost 50% is spent on arms. This irrational imbalance has led to all public health institutions having to work with equipment that is totally obsolete and often barely able to function. There is a universal shortage of medicines and materials, while remote and rural areas have virtually no access to any sort of healthcare. Moreover, it is precisely in those regions that there has been a dramatic rise in cases of malaria, HIV/Aids and tuberculosis, though the regime publicly denies it.

Things are scarcely any better in the field of education. Officially just 10% of the population are said to be illiterate, but only one child in two finishes primary school, and only one in three goes on to secondary education. In rural and ethnic minority regions, the number of people who leave school early is much higher. Since the 1990s, universities have been closed more and more frequently in order to prevent students from engaging in political activities.

Burma's currency is the kyat, and the official exchange rate is 6 kyats to the US dollar. On the black market, which is used by everybody, the rate is 1,000 kyats to the dollar.

Discontinued kyat notes showing the Burmese national hero Aung San

Past and Present အတိတ် နဲ့ ပစ္စုပွန်

Early Settlers

Throughout its history, Burma has experienced waves of immigration that have come southwards along the rivers Irrawaddy (Ayeyarwady), Chindwin, Salween (Thanlwin) and Mekong. These movements have brought in many different ethnic peoples, mainly from the Central Asian plateau (modern Tibet and China), and this is reflected in the wide ethnic variety to be found in the country today. As in many other parts of South-East Asia, the early inhabitants were probably Negritos, but were driven out by the tribal peoples that came in from the north.

The first historically recorded inhabitants were the Mon, who from the 6th century BC settled all over the south, in the Irrawaddy Delta and along the Gulf of Martaban (Mottama), as well as along the Chao Phraya River in modern-day Thailand. The Mon had flourishing cultural and economic links with India, and it was through these that Buddhism made its way into Burma. Legend has it that the mysterious land of Suvarnabhumi (or 'Golden Land'), mentioned in numerous ancient sources and the subject of much debate, was in fact the homeland of the Mon, who established their first kingdom in Burma in c. 300 BC around the port of Thaton, which developed into an important trading centre.

From the first century AD, the Pyus settled in central Burma. They were also quick to espouse Buddhism, and they founded highly civilized city-kingdoms which, at their peak, during the 7th and 8th centuries, also became prosperous trading centres. The largest city was Sri Ksetra, close to present-day Prome (Pyay). It is believed that the first Karen and Chin provided the next wave of immigrants to central Burma, before the Burmese came from Tibet during the 8th and 9th centuries. They overthrew the Pyus, and spread out along the trade routes of the Irrawaddy which the Pyus had previously controlled. At around the same time, the first Shan immigrants entered Burma from the kingdom of Nan Chao (Yunnan Province, China).

The Burmese Kingdoms

In 849, the Burmese established the important kingdom of Pagan (Bagan) around the old Pyu city of Pukam. The power of this kingdom was strengthened in 1057 when the ruling monarch King Anawrahta conquered the Mon and captured their capital Thaton, thereby gaining access to the important harbours in the Gulf of Martaban and the Andaman Sea. Furthermore, by forcibly abducting 30,000 educated Mon, Pagan had at its disposal a large enough trained workforce to turn the city into an outstanding cultural and spiritual centre for the next 250 years. The sacred Buddhist writings of the *Pali Canon* – the best-known version of the *Tipitaka*, the sacred canon of Theravada Buddhism – were also taken from the kingdom of the Mon, and these led to the adoption of Theravada Buddhism as the main religion of the Burmese – a faith that found its expression in the masterly architecture of some 13,000 temples and pagodas. Initially it was the Mon language and script that had most influence over the culture of the Burmese, but at the beginning of the 12th century they developed their own script. Although the kingdom experienced a steady decline following Anawrahta's death, this first Burmese dynasty was one of the most significant periods in the country's history.

In 1287 the Mongol emperor Kublai Khan invaded, angered by King Narathihapate's refusal to pay tribute to him and the assassination of his Mongolian ambassadors. His armies destroyed Pagan – and with it, political unity. The Mon were able to break free of Burmese control and re-establish themselves in the south of Burma. However, from this point on, the Shan came in increasing numbers from the north, taking over the Burmese territories and establishing their own states. During the centuries that followed, the Shan and the Mon were in constant conflict with one another, which enabled the Burmese to build up their strength again. They gradually extended their power north and south, conquering the respective Shan and Mon capitals of Ava (Inwa) and Pegu (Bago), and established the Second Burmese Empire, which lasted from 1531 until 1752. During this period, the Burmese kingdom enjoyed its greatest expansion, which even extended beyond the present borders to the Indian state of Manipur (conquered in 1560), and the Siamese kingdoms of Lanna (Chiang Mai) and Ayutthaya (1569) in present-day Thailand.

The Mon rose up against the Burmese for the last time in 1752 and captured Ava, but their triumph was short-lived. In the same year, the Burmese King Alaungpaya regained control, and when he conquered the Mon kingdom of Pegu in 1757, he secured his power over central and southern Burma. Many Mon fled across the border to Siam, while others integrated with the Burmese. This conquest marked the beginning of the Third Burmese Empire, the Konbaung dynasty. In 1767 Ayutthaya was once again the target of Burmese attacks, and this time the royal Siamese city was so comprehensively demolished that it was necessary to build a new capital – Bangkok. These historic events have left a deep scar on the collective memory of the Thais.

The Colonial Era

In 1784, the Burmese under King Bodawpaya conquered the western regions and annexed the mighty kingdom of Arakan (Rakhine). The Burmese empire now stretched as far as the Indian border, where the British colonial masters looked on with extreme unease. After the Burmese King Bagyidaw conquered Assam and Manipur in 1819, the First Anglo-Burmese war broke out, lasting from 1824 until 1826, at the end of which the British took control of the region. With the Treaty of Yandabo, Bagyidaw was forced to cede the occupied Indian provinces together with Arakan and the coastal strip of Tenasserim (Tanintharyi) to the British.

There followed repeated and bloody struggles over succession within the royal house itself, which led to a slow decline in the Konbaung dynasty. The British seized on this weakness, and in 1852 used the fining of two British sea captains over import-duty violations as a pretext for declaring war again. This time they were able to annex the whole of southern Burma – subsequently known as Lower Burma – to British India.

One year later, Prince Mindon overthrew his half-brother King Pagan, who had been defeated by the British, and had himself crowned King in Amarapura, moving the capital to Mandalay in 1857. During his twenty-five-year reign, Mindon sought to improve relations with the British, and step-by-step he led his country into the modern economic age. However, when the great King Mindon died in 1878, the golden age of his capital city Mandalay came to an abrupt end. In constant fear of assassination, he had failed to name a successor, and so his death sparked a violent struggle for the

Nineteenth-century postcard of Sampan Pagoda, Shwegyin, Pegu Division

throne. Thanks to the intrigues of his future mother-in-law, the totally inexperienced Thibaw finally became the last King of Burma in 1878. His policies were largely dictated by his ambitious wife Supalayat and some equally power-hungry government ministers, under whose influence relations with the British swiftly deteriorated. Once again, in 1885, the colonial masters used a harmless dispute over trading concessions to justify waging war on Burma. This time they succeeded in conquering the whole country, and the King and his family were driven out of the palace in Mandalay and sent into exile in Ratnagiri, India. In 1886 Burma lost its independence and became yet another province in the British colony of India, with Rangoon as its new capital.

Resistance to British Occupation

The Burmese people staged many violent protests against the foreign invaders, who initially found it extremely difficult to keep the country under control. Only when the ancient Roman principle of *divide et impera* was implemented did the colony eventually calm down. The British were adept at winning over the ethnic minorities by separating their regions from the rest of the country as so-called 'frontier areas', and then giving the ethnic peoples certain privileges, such as the right to keep their royal titles. In central Burma, however, they established a colonial administration. Furthermore, the fact that apart from Britons and Indians, only members of non-Burmese ethnic groups were allowed to enter the army created much resentment among the Burmese, and fanned the flames of an ethnic conflict that is still ongoing.

Kachin women in traditional dress

In the early 20th century, following the example of Mahatma Gandhi's fight for independence in India, the Burmese mounted demonstrations and campaigns of civil disobedience, and it was often the monks and students who led the rebellion against the colonial masters. In 1930 the *Thakin* (Masters) movement was founded, and among its members was a young man called Aung San who later came to the forefront in the long students' strikes of 1936.

In 1941, as the Second World War progressed and the Japanese advanced into Asia, Aung San and several comrades-in-arms whom he had personally selected travelled to the island of Hainan (China), where they were given military training by the Japanese. The so-called Thirty Comrades included U Nu and Ne Win, who were to make a lasting mark on the history of Burma during the decades that followed. Together with the Japanese army, Aung San's newly formed Burma Independence Army (BIA) fought against the British and American forces, whose soldiers were not used to the demands of jungle warfare.

On 8 March 1942, the capital Rangoon was captured, and it seemed as if at last the colonial rulers were about to be driven out. But the Japanese liberators, who had initially been greeted with a rapturous welcome, soon turned out to be even more brutal and repressive than their British predecessors. Even the formal declaration of independence on 1 August 1943 and the appointment of Ba Maw as prime minister could not mask Japan's colonial ambitions. As a result, the Burmese nationalist movement switched allegiance and at the beginning of 1944 offered to support the British in their efforts to reconquer Burma, on condition that the country should then be granted full independence.

The Allies, with active help from Aung San's Anti-Fascist People's Freedom League (AFPFL), succeeded in recapturing Rangoon from the Japanese in May 1945. The Japanese occupying forces had no support from the Burmese people, whom they had so brutally repressed, and the multicultural guerrilla units of the British Army – named the 'Chindits' – inflicted heavy losses on them before they finally surrendered in August 1945.

With the election of Clement Attlee as Britain's prime minister in 1945, the process of decolonization took on an ever-clearer shape. At the beginning of 1947, Aung San and Attlee signed an agreement in London that guaranteed the future of a united Burma to include all its ethnic groups. With the legendary Panglong Agreement of 12 February 1947, Aung San and the ethnic peoples of Kachin, Chin and Shan agreed to join the newly established Union of Burma for a period of ten years (see pages 147–48).

The Murder of Aung San and the Ne Win Regime

In the elections of April 1947, the AFPFL won its expected victory, but it was not long before the political and ethnic divisions in the country made their presence felt in dramatic fashion. On 19 July, Aung San and six other members of the constitutional committee were assassinated. Burma's national hero did not live to see his country's hard-won independence granted on 4 January 1948. U Nu replaced him at the head of the AFPFL and became the country's first prime minister, and the Shan prince Sao Shwe Thaike was elected president.

After the assassination of Aung San, the first few years of this new state were marked by a great deal of political instability. Without his charismatic leadership, the Panglong Agreement lost its binding force, and with it went his dream of friendly coexistence between all the ethnic groups living in Burma under the guiding principle of 'Unity in Diversity'. In 1949 Burma saw the beginning of one of the longest civil wars in world history, as the Karen and later the other ethnic minorities launched their campaign for freedom and autonomy. The Communist Party of Burma (CPB) also took up arms against the government. After the rebel forces initially succeeded in capturing large areas of the country and even penetrated as far as Rangoon, General Ne Win's Burmese Army (known as the *Tatmadaw*) – with ruthless brutality even against the ethnic civilian population – drove them back mainly to the border regions.

In 1962, when prime minister U Nu began to negotiate with the rebels, in order to bring the civil war to an end, the military leader Ne Win staged a coup. The official reason given was his desire to maintain the Union of Burma, and in order to achieve this – amid talk of Burma's independent road to Socialism – he deemed it necessary to have members of the government arrested and to abolish the multi-party system. The only party allowed was the Burma Socialist Programme Party (BSPP). Banks, industries and trading companies were nationalized, and the country found itself for the most part internationally isolated. A hundred thousand Indian settlers, who were mainly engaged in commerce, were expelled from Burma, and during the next few decades this extraordinarily brutal military regime was to deprive the people of many of their basic human rights.

Burma Today

Since the 1980s, the junta's catastrophic mishandling of the economy, which has resulted in Burma losing its status as one of the world's major exporters of rice, has plunged the country into an appalling economic crisis. In 1988, the situation reached fever pitch and, in August of that year, students staged a national strike. Many demonstrators swarmed through the

Kuthodaw Pagoda,
Mandalay, *c.* 1900

streets, until heavily armed soldiers arrived, shooting at random into the crowds. During this period, thousands of students, activists, monks, women and children were murdered all over the country after what had been the largest demonstration so far against the dictatorship, with many fleeing over the border to neighbouring Thailand.

The most significant opposition to the junta was established during these turbulent months: the National League for Democracy (NLD), whose General Secretary and co-founder is Aung San Suu Kyi, the daughter of the national hero Aung San. In the aftermath of the demonstrations, during which some individual members of the military had joined in the protests and made contact with the political opposition, there was another coup, with defence minister and commander-in-chief General Saw Maung seizing power. He then set up the State Law & Order Restoration Council (SLORC). One of the first actions undertaken by the Council, in 1989, was to rename Burma the 'Union of Myanmar' and also to give new names to many of the towns and rivers. The former capital is no longer Rangoon but Yangon. The official reason was that this would enable the regime to incorporate all the ethnic groups into the union, thus making a clean break with the colonial past. In actual fact, the people have continued to use the name Burma in conversation, and only refer to Myanmar in official contexts, as historically both words have been used to refer to the majority ethnic group rather than the country. The whole affair can be dismissed solely as propaganda, and the opposition as well as the regime's opponents all over the world refer to the country almost exclusively by its former name.

International pressure forced the junta to hold free elections in 1990, and these resulted in a landslide victory for the NLD. Although the NLD won over 82% of the 485 contested seats in parliament, the military refused to hand over power, and instead have continued since 1993 to work on a 'Constitution'. The constitutional national assembly is a charade, since the only delegates appointed are those who are loyal to the regime, thus perpetuating the special privileges that the military have given themselves. For this reason, many representatives of the opposition parties, including the NLD, have long since refused to take part in the masquerade that calls itself the National Convention. In May 2008, a national referendum was held in order to pass the Constitution. During the process, Burmese troops forced villagers in the border regions at gun-point to vote in favour of it. This whole election could be seen as a deliberate attempt to dupe the international community, and the result was established by undemocratic means. There are strict limits on political activity, as in all such autocracies. Countless activists have been arrested, imprisoned and tortured during the last twenty years, and at present there are believed to be more than 2,100 political prisoners in Burma. Since 1989, the charismatic leader of the democratic movement and Nobel Peace Prize winner Aung San Suu Kyi has been kept almost permanently under house arrest (see pages 176–77).

In order to rescue the economy, the military decided at the beginning of the 1990s to end the country's isolation. Lucrative attractions for foreign exchange included abundant natural resources such as teak, oil and gas, and these were duly exploited on a large scale. Tourism was another important means of earning hard currency, and so 1996 was declared 'Visit Myanmar Year'. The regime projected 500,000 visitors a year, but this target has never looked like being reached. With a view to improving Burma's infrastructure so that it could cope with the expected flood of foreign visitors, the authorities fell back on the tried and trusted method of forced labour. Hundreds of thousands of people, including children, were set to work – with no remuneration – building roads, railways, hotels and airports. Towns and villages were relocated to ensure that the tourists never got to see the terrible living conditions of their inhabitants – Pagan being a prime example.

After the massacres of 1988, the West – in particular the USA and the EU – decided to impose more or less rigid sanctions on Burma. The EU restricted itself to relatively trivial measures against the regime, and they have had little effect: for instance, the personal accounts held by members of the government in EU banks were frozen, but this did not apply to the accounts of the commercial enterprises owned by the junta. Since Burma is also economically geared to its mighty neighbour China, the potential impact of Western boycotts is negligible in any case. ASEAN, to which Burma has belonged since 1997, prefers to follow a policy of non-intervention in the affairs of other states, and especially China, Russia and Ukraine do not regard the Burmese government's constant violations of human rights as a reason for stopping arms supplies.

Life in Burma is a mixture of fear and stagnation. By exercising total control over its people, the government seeks to impose discipline and submission in order to consolidate its own power. It has also encouraged increasing devotion to Buddhism: by building magnificent new pagodas, the junta aims to improve its karma and to create an atmosphere of calm acceptance in the population. The media is used to exploit any and every contact with nationally respected monks. Following the pro-democracy protests of 2007, during which hundreds of demonstrators were arrested or murdered, including many monks, the image of the government took a major turn for the worse both abroad and at home, but not even this seems to have had any effect on the regime. Even during the catastrophic cyclone, which hit the Irrawaddy Delta on 3 May 2008, the junta showed the population no sign of support and blocked the international relief effort during the first three weeks. Almost 100,000 were killed by Cyclone Nargis and 2 million were made homeless, but the junta's only concern was in stopping foreign journalists from covering the disaster and in cementing its grip on power by ploughing ahead with the undemocratic constitutional referendum one week later.

Recently more and more rumours have been circulating about the delicate health of General Than Shwe, long-time leader of the State Peace & Development Council (SPDC), which became the new name for SLORC in 1997. However, it seems unlikely, even if he were to step down, that there would be any real change in favour of democracy. The political situation is simply too confused, with a stifled opposition and divers rebel groups that have comparatively little in the way of military equipment. Diplomatic pressure is also doomed to failure without a unified international policy. It seems that Burma can only remain trapped, as it has been for so long, in a political cul de sac.

Overleaf, clockwise from top left: many Kayan women wear brass rings; pagoda, Pagan, Mandalay Division; palm juice extraction, Pagan; overcrowded pick-up truck, Yawnghwe, Shan State; roadside food stalls and tearooms, a common meeting point in Burma; traditional weaving, Lake Inle, Shan State; religious parade, Lashio, Shan State

Rangoon (Yangon) ရန်ကုန်

With a little luck, you will be able to see the symbol of Rangoon as you fly towards the city: the venerable and hugely impressive Shwedagon Pagoda, rising in glorious gold from its green hill and seeming to stand guard over the great metropolis. Although Rangoon was the capital of Burma for little more than a hundred years, its roots go back many centuries. Built on the site of the ancient Mon city of Dagon, which is thought to have been founded more than 2,000 years ago, it lies along the Rangoon River and is one of the country's major ports. The little fishing village was given the name Yangon (meaning 'end of strife') by King Alaungpaya following his conquest of the Mon kingdom of Pegu in 1757, and in 1886 was renamed Rangoon by the British when Burma was annexed as a crown colony.

The influence of the former colonial masters is still to be seen in the layout: the inner city is organized like a chessboard, and many of the old Victorian buildings have survived in varying states of preservation. Since the country was opened up in the mid-1990s, more and more modern buildings have been erected, mainly apartment blocks and shopping centres. This architectural mixture of the old and new, many already looking somewhat the worse for wear, lends the city a fascinating aura of its own.

At first sight this metropolis, with its population of 5 million, seems much more leisurely than other great cities in Asia. There are comparatively few cars, and it is mainly pedestrians and *trishaws* (Burmese cycle rickshaws) that fill the streets. A wide variety of cultures and religions mingle together, and the innumerable Buddhist pagodas stand side-by-side with Hindu temples, mosques and churches. Many Indians and Chinese have settled here, running businesses and living in their own quarters of the city.

Rangoon welcomes its visitors with a mixture of strange smells coming from all the roadside tearooms and hot food stalls, which are very popular with the local

Pages 22–23:
Shwedagon Pagoda

Preceding pages, clockwise from top left: Sule Pagoda; (above) Bogyoke Aung San Museum, former home of Aung San; (below) Rangoon City Hall; Anawrahta Road; water stall; bus conductor; street market, Botahtaung township

Opposite:
Konzaydan Street, downtown Rangoon

Below: Rangoon Division

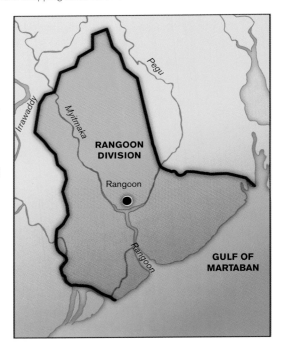

inhabitants. At every corner you will find people sitting on tiny plastic chairs at small tables, sipping tea or nibbling their snacks. There's plenty of hustle and bustle, and a constant hubbub of loud voices as the street vendors offer their wares. At the bus stops people scramble for places in the ancient, rickety, overloaded buses that rumble their stately way through the streets.

At the heart of the old city, in the middle of a roundabout, stands the **Sule Pagoda**. It is believed to be over 2,000 years old, although no one really knows exactly when it was built, and its octagonal stupa is said to contain a hair of the Buddha. This pagoda is used by the faithful mainly to offer up prayers for everyday problems, and thanks to its central position it is in constant use. Immediately south-east of the Sule Pagoda is the small Mahabandoola Park, which contains the **Independence Monument** – a large obelisk guarded by statues of *chinthes*, mythical lions.

There are lots of markets all over the city, offering a wide variety of local wares such as spices and textiles, together with goods imported mainly from China and Thailand. The largest of these is the **Bogyoke Aung San Market**, where one can find Burmese handicrafts as well as precious stones from the north, such as rubies and jade. There are also plenty of money changers who offer far more kyats to the dollar than any of the local banks.

If you want to relax, go to **Lake Kandawgyi**, to the north of the city. The large expanse of green and the many restaurants all around the lake create an idyllic atmosphere well worth the trip. Another sight worth seeing is the **Bogyoke Aung San Museum**, which is very close to the lake in Bahan township. This is the former home of the national hero Aung San and his wife. The furniture and fittings have been left exactly as they were during his lifetime, and on the walls are old family photos. Visitors can even see the room of his famous daughter Aung San Suu Kyi, although her name will never be mentioned during an official guided tour.

Shwedagon Pagoda

ရွှေတိဂုံ စေတီတော်

'Then, a golden mystery upheaved itself on the horizon – a beautiful, winking wonder that blazed in the sun, of a shape that was neither Muslim dome nor Hindu temple spire. It stood upon a green knoll… "There's the old Shway Dagon," said my companion… The golden dome said, "This is Burma, and it will be quite unlike any land you know about."'
Rudyard Kipling, *Letters from the East*, 1889

The **Shwedagon Pagoda** is not only the religious centre of Rangoon, but it is also the cultural and spiritual heart of Burma itself. Buddhists come on pilgrimages from all over the country to this historic site, to venerate the Buddha and to breathe in the meditative spirit of this sacred shrine, and visitors are enchanted by its shining golden beauty.

Although the precise origins of the pagoda are unclear, legend has it that more than 2,500 years ago two merchants, the brothers Taphussa and Bhallika, heard about a famine in neighbouring Bengal and headed west with 500 oxcarts laden with rice. On their way they met a *nat* spirit, who asked them if they wanted gold or the treasures of heaven. After they had opted for the latter, the *nat* took them to the Lord Buddha, who was sitting meditating under a sacred tree. The brothers offered honey cake to the Enlightened One, and as a reward they were given eight of his hairs, which they were to take home to the sacred site of Singuttara Hill. On their return journey they had to give two of these hairs to King Ajjhata and two more to the Naga King Jayasena. But when Taphussa and Bhallika, together with King Okkalapa, took the remaining hairs to Singuttara Hill, miraculously they found all eight hairs in the casket. Gautama Buddha's hairs were placed in a chamber that was knee-deep in jewels, alongside relics of the three preceding Buddhas: Kakusandha's staff, Konagamana's water filter, and a piece of Kassapa's robe. One after another, stupas of gold, silver, copper, bronze, iron, marble and finally brick were erected over the shrine to a height of approximately 10 metres (33 ft).

Over the centuries, the ancient pagoda has suffered significant damage from earthquakes, and has been continuously reconstructed and extended by successive rulers. The tradition of gilding the stupa was begun in the 15th century by Queen Shin Saw Bu, who provided her body weight in gold, and was continued by subsequent rulers, and even today pilgrims decorate it with gold leaf. An estimated 60 tonnes of gold is thought to adorn the pagoda, which now rises 98 metres (322 ft) above its base and covers a vast area. In addition, at the top of the stupa is a *hti* (umbrella) which is

During the Light Festival, which marks the end of Buddhist Lent, worshippers light candles at the Shwedagon Pagoda

believed to contain more than 7,000 diamonds, rubies and sapphires and can be seen sparkling in the sun for miles around.

On all four sides of the 60,000 square metre (646,000 ft^2) complex there are covered stairways to the marble platform on which the pagoda stands, each guarded by two *chinthes*. Along these steps are vendors selling devotional objects and souvenirs. In the middle of the platform stands the main stupa, surrounded by four large and sixty-four smaller stupas. Among the many structures surrounding the central stupa on the platform are shrines flanked by planetary posts, each dedicated to a different day of the week, and here people who were born on those days offer up their prayers and pour water over the Buddha and the appropriate animal. Next to the Kakusandha shrine, for instance – the first shrine you encounter if approaching from the eastern stairway – is the planetary post for the Moon where people who were born on a Monday, and whose animal sign is the tiger, gather. From the many pavilions comes the soft murmuring of prayers, and whole families congregate to meditate or picnic in the areas devoted to the last four Buddhas of our age. Offerings are made to *nat* spirits and to the enshrined images of venerated monks, and one can also see columns of the faithful busily sweeping, in the hope of improving their karma by means of this communal work.

Quite apart from its spiritual importance for the entire nation, the Shwedagon Pagoda also mirrors political turning-points in the history of Burma. It was here, for instance, that students gathered in 1920 to protest against their British colonial rulers, and it was here that freedom fighter Aung San and later his daughter Aung San Suu Kyi, the present leader of the opposition, held their first speeches, delivered to ecstatic audiences. It was also at this holy site that the monks began their protest march in September 2007.

Irrawaddy Division

Bassein (Pathein) ပုသိမ်

Pages 36–37:
Irrawaddy riverbank

Preceding pages:
Bassein, from top
left: Shwemokhtaw
Pagoda; *pathein hti*
umbrella; St Peter's
Cathedral; boy at
the Twenty-Eight
[Buddhas] Pagoda;
flower stall; ferry
passenger

Opposite: (above)
pathein hti;
(below) market
scene, Bassein

Below: Irrawaddy
Division

The largest city in the Irrawaddy Delta, with a population of about 300,000, is Bassein which lies along the river of the same name. The most leisurely way to approach this city is by boat. From Rangoon – which lies around 160 kilometres (99 mi) to the east of Bassein – the ferry takes at least eighteen hours, passing deep into the delta region through narrow canals and rivers. Green mangrove forests and muddy shores alternate with fishing villages and small towns whose inhabitants seem to spend their entire lives either beside or on the water.

The delta is a very fertile area, and rice especially has been cultivated here since the colonial era, when the British drained the swamplands and made them suitable for agriculture. The significant trade in rice exports has helped the area to prosper and transformed Bassein into one of the country's most important delta ports, despite its distance from the sea. With over 6 million inhabitants, most of them Burmese and Karen, this is the most densely populated area in the whole of Burma. The ecosystem of the mangroves also provides a habitat for many endangered species, including the largest reptile in the world, the saltwater crocodile.

During the first millennium, the Mon developed the port of Bassein into a major trading centre for goods from China and India, and many Muslim traders settled there. Today the deep-water port is the biggest trading place for high-quality rice from the delta region.

In addition the town is best known for its fine bamboo umbrellas (*pathein hti*), which have been made by successive generations of family craftsmen. You can observe various phases of the long-drawn-out process in a number of small workshops, and then you will be faced with the torture of choosing which umbrella you are going to take home as a souvenir. The dark red ones are a common sight all over Burma because the monks are particularly fond of using them as protection from the sun.

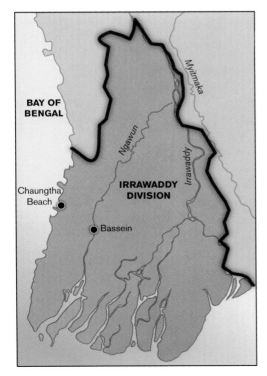

BAY OF
BENGAL

Ngawun

Myitmaka

Irrawaddy

Chaungtha
Beach

**IRRAWADDY
DIVISION**

Bassein

Shwemokhtaw Pagoda ရွှေမော်ခေါ် ဘုရား

The primary landmark in Bassein is the **Shwemokhtaw Pagoda**, opposite the central market. Its origins, though shrouded in legend, are linked to the Indian emperor Ashoka, who reigned in the 3rd century BC. The original ancient stupa, which stood just over two metres (7ft) tall, is said to have contained Buddha relics and a 6-inch (15-cm) gold bar, and it is from this legend that the Shwemokhtaw Pagoda (meaning 'Stupa of the Half-foot Gold Bar') takes its name. A taller stupa is believed to have been erected on the site in the 12th century, and in the 13th century the structure was raised further by the Mon King Samodagossa and given its present name. The shape of the stupa has remained virtually unchanged since Samodagossa's time, but additions to the richly ornamented *hti* at the top of the structure – decorated with gold, diamonds and rubies – have increased the height of the pagoda to 47 metres (154 ft).

The Shwemokhtaw Pagoda also contains a much venerated figure of the Buddha which is said to have originated in Sri Lanka and to have been washed ashore on a raft. Legend has it that four Buddhas were sculpted from pieces of the Bodhi Tree, the ancient fig tree in Bodh Gaya, India, under which Siddhartha Gautama attained Enlightenment, and were then set adrift on the sea. The Buddha image now housed in the Shwemokhtaw Pagoda is said to have landed near the fishing village of Phondawpyi, almost 100 kilometres (62 mi) south of Bassein, before being brought to the city by the Mon Queen Shin Saw Bu in the 15th century.

Near the pagoda are several markets, offering all sorts of delights for the adventurous tourist's tastebuds. It is perhaps the large night market on Strand Road that has the most interesting array of goods, and wandering among its many stalls, all loaded with food and other everyday items, makes for an interesting promenade. You can also watch regional specialities being prepared and cooked there.

Opposite: (above) hustle and bustle outside the Shwemokhtaw Pagoda; (below left) the Shwemokhtaw stupa; (below right) a religious statue at the pagoda

Arakan State

Arakan State (Rakhine State) ရခိုင်ပြည်နယ်

Pages 44–45:
Htukkanthein
Temple, Myohaung

Preceding pages,
clockwise from left:
Buddha statues
near the Kothaung
Temple, Myohaung;
young cowherd;
fruits at Myohaung's
market; oxcart laden
with harvest

Opposite:
Theindaung Pagoda,
Myohaung

Below: Arakan State

Arakan State lies in western Burma, on the border with Bangladesh. With its unusual geographical features, this remote region occupies a special place in Burma. The barely accessible Arakan-Yoma mountains, which rise to a height of 3,000 metres (8,843 ft), separate the state from the rest of the country. Direct access to the Bay of Bengal offers magnificent, almost untouched beaches along the coast, but during the monsoon season the region is subject to the heaviest rainfall in Burma. May, October and November are especially prone to violent storms.

Most of the islands are military zones from which tourists are banned. As Arakan contains many rivers but a very poor road network, plane and boat are the most common forms of transport. Unofficially, the population is estimated at around 2.7 million. In addition to the Arakanese, who are descended from the original Negrito inhabitants and are mainly Buddhist, there are numerous small ethnic groups as well as a large number of Muslim Rohingya. These are descendants of Arab and Bengali traders, soldiers and refugees who settled here in the 7th century AD. Arakan served as a bridge between South and South-East Asia, and the many

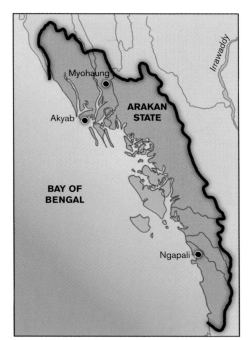

different ethnic peoples and cultures all left their mark. In the course of its more recent history, it was an autonomous kingdom under alternating Hindu, Buddhist and Muslim rule. Even Ptolemy had heard of it – he mentions it in his writings (AD 150) under the name of Argyre ('Silver Land').

During the first millennium AD, Arakan was ruled by Indian Hindus and it functioned as the subcontinent's gateway to the east. At that time, Buddhism was already widespread in the region, and it is said that the Buddha himself travelled through Arakan in the 6th century BC. Legend has it that the most venerated figure in Burma, the Mahamuni Buddha, was cast during this visit after the Buddha's true image, although archaeologists believe that the bronze statue was erected in the 2nd century AD in Dhanyawady, close to the former capital Myohaung (Mrauk U). The coastal region, with its many ports and estuaries, became

a significant trading centre for Arabian and Chinese merchants and
seafarers en route to China. In 1057 Arakan was conquered by the
Burmese King Anawrahta and annexed to the mighty Pagan empire,
but thanks to its isolated geographical situation it still retained much
of its independence.

The great kingdom of Bengal became Muslim in 1203, which had
significant cultural and political effects on the little neighbouring state in
the east. From 1430, Arakan itself became a kingdom, though as a vassal
state it initially still had to pay taxes to the Bengali sultan; not until 1531
did it become fully autonomous. From then on, it was traditional for the
kings to bear Muslim titles in addition to their Arakanese names, and
generally the region was dominated by Islam, adopting its culture and
customs. Arakan marked the easternmost frontier of Islamic expansion
by land – largely owing to the insurmountable barrier of the Arakan-Yoma
mountains. During the 16th century, with the aid of Portuguese soldiers
and sailors, King Min Bin of the Myohaung dynasty built up an army of
foreign and native mercenaries and a fleet of 10,000 ships, and in 1538
he conquered parts of East Bengal (now Bangladesh).

Above: Arakanese
fisherman, Kaladan
River

Opposite: (above)
many Burmese
women put *thanakha*
yellow paste on their
faces as a form of
sunblock; (below)
Arakanese-style
bronze Buddha
statue

The recapture of Chittagong (now Bangladesh) by the Mughal empire in 1666 began the decline and fall of the Myohaung dynasty. There followed many years of political instability, with a rapid succession of kings who reigned for very short periods, until Arakan was finally annexed by the Burmese King Bodawpaya in 1784. He immediately set about destroying everything Muslim, both material and cultural, and took the Mahamuni Buddha as a trophy back to Mandalay, where it has remained to this day. All of this led to lasting tensions between the Muslims and the Buddhists.

Since 1948, and especially after the military coup in 1962, the Rohingya have increasingly fallen victim to discrimination and repression at the hands of the Burmese government and the Arakanese due to their religion and ethnic origin. The military regime does not regard them as an indigenous people but as migrants from India, and it is continually trying to drive them out of Burma by means of harassment or direct attack. Like many members of other minority groups, they are subject to murder, rape, torture and forced labour. Many of them speak of ethnic cleansing, and as a result more than a million Rohingya have fled to neighbouring Bangladesh, Pakistan or India.

Myohaung (Mrauk U) မြို့ဟောင်း

The former capital of the kingdom of Arakan can only be reached by ship – foreigners are not allowed to travel overland. From Akyab (Sittwe) you sail inland for about six hours along the Kaladan River, past endless fields of rice and grazing water buffalo. Modern technology does not seem to have penetrated very far into this region, and there is no electricity or running water in the simple huts of the farmers and fishermen who live on the banks of the river. There are swarms of bright little sailing boats going up and down the river, hunting for fish, and now and then a dilapidated old freighter or passenger ship will come chugging towards you, briefly breaking the otherwise peaceful harmony of the enchanting landscape.

Myohaung was established as the Arakanese capital by King Min Saw Mon in 1430, and it quickly developed into an important centre for trade, handicrafts and art, with links to Europe and Arabia. This lively and impressive city, with 30 kilometres (19 mi) of defensive walls and a strategic position between mountains and rivers, was well nigh impregnable for 350 years, and in the 17th century Dutch sailors even compared it to London and Amsterdam. From 1629 onwards the Portuguese Augustine missionary Sebastião Manrique lived for several years in the city, which then had a population of 160,000, and wrote in glowing terms of the splendid court and the wealth that was evident everywhere. Only when the British occupation began in 1826 and the seat of administration was moved to Akyab did Myohaung lose its pre-eminent position.

Today Myohaung is a small, quiet town with a large number of pagodas and temples scattered all around. Unlike the people of Pagan, the inhabitants are still living among these religious edifices and have so far escaped expulsion. On almost every hill you will see sandstone pagodas in varying degrees of decay. Tourists are a rarity here and are treated by the locals with a mixture of sceptical reserve and cheerful curiosity. If you wander through the outlying villages, you will find yourself being seen as a rare attraction, particularly by the many children, who will greet you with loud voices and watch you intently. Everyday life seems almost archaic, with water drawn from the well, and the main forms of transport being bicycles and oxcarts.

The most important sight is the **Shittaung Pagoda**, which means the 'Shrine of the 80,000 Buddhas'. The interior actually contains no fewer

Opposite: (above) Shittaung Pagoda, Myohaung; (below) residents draw water from a nearby well

than 84,000 figures and reliefs of the Buddha. It was built in a single year (1535) on the orders of King Min Bin, shortly after his successful defence against Portuguese invaders, and this victory is commemorated by its alternative name: Ran Aung Zeya ('Temple of Victory').

In the great memorial hall, one of the many sculptures is a 3-metre-high (10-ft) Buddha seated on a throne. The dark winding passages that branch off from this hall are full of images of the Buddha, some painted and others artistically carved into the walls, and there are also scenes of court life, dancers and battles. The *Jataka* (the story of the Buddha's different births) is told in a series of 550 reliefs. A few years ago the pagoda was restored, but with a sad lack of sensitivity, for its exterior is now a miserable grey that is reminiscent of military barracks.

A few metres to the north of the Shittaung Pagoda stands the **Andaw Pagoda**, built in 1521 by King Min Hla Raza. It is said to contain one of the Buddha's teeth, which King Min Bin brought from Sri Lanka. The octagonal main temple is surrounded by sixteen smaller, round stupas.

Directly opposite is another highlight: the **Htukkanthein Temple**. This fortress-like building was erected in 1571 by King Min Phalaung and has an impressive covered walkway inside the bell-shaped stupa which is lined with more than one hundred stone sculptures of the Buddha, as well as images of ordinary people. At the end of this spiralling walkway, which encircles the centre almost three times, is a prayer hall in which sits another, much venerated figure of the Buddha.

Close to the market, in the centre of the town, there was once a majestic **royal palace**. Built of teak, and covered with gold, the grounds of this royal residence are said to have contained gardens, fountains and artificial lakes. Sadly, the only remnants of its former glories are the ruins of its crumbling foundation walls. The museum, on the other hand, is well worth a visit. On display are a large number of archaeological artefacts from different periods of the Arakan empire.

In the north-east of the town, a little further away from the central cluster of pagodas, is the **Kothaung Temple**. It can be reached on foot along a sandy track which runs beside rich green fields and small lakes. With this temple, built in 1553, King Min Tikkha wanted to outdo his father Min Bin (who built the Shittaung Pagoda) by immortalizing the Buddha 90,000 times. This is reflected in the name Kothaung, which means 'Shrine of the 90,000 Buddhas'. On the upper level of this gradually decaying, rectangular building are crowds of sculptures of different sizes, some of them restored, but it is on the lower level that you will find the majority of the images, carved into the walls of the circular walkway.

Opposite: (above) Kothaung Temple, Myohaung; (below) Buddha-lined vaults of the Shittaung Pagoda

Ngapali Beach ငပလီ

The long, golden beaches along the Arakan coastline are among the most beautiful in the world and attract more and more tourists every year. Ngapali, in the south of the state, is Burma's most popular beach destination, and yet this remarkably unspoilt spot manages to retain an almost empty, exclusive feel, in sharp contrast to the many crowded beaches of neighbouring Thailand. Here, dreams of idyllic palm-fringed beaches, lapped by crystal-clear tropical waters, merge with reality.

The accommodation on offer at Ngapali caters to all price brackets and ranges from homely bungalows to luxury spa resorts. The hotel complexes in particular, which are heavily promoted by the travel agencies, are designed to fulfil visitors' very possible desire. Often only the richest Burmese are to be found here, and indeed until a few years ago only the military and their relatives were allowed to holiday at Ngapali Beach.

Every now and then oxcarts can be seen meandering along the beach and have become a popular photo opportunity among tourists, especially at sunset. At the southern end of the beach there is a little fishing village where you can wander around freely and watch all the comings and

Idyllic scenes such as these have made Ngapali a popular destination

goings. In the morning there is a flurry of activity as the weary fishermen return and unload the day's catch. All around the village you will see the small fish laid out on plastic tarpaulins to dry in the sun before being sold at the market.

Another landmark is the bizarre rock formation at the northern tip of the beach which looks like solid lava and juts out into the sea. Keen snorkellers will enjoy exploring the rich, colourful sea life, and it is also possible to take boat trips to the surrounding islands.

Mandalay Division and Mingun

Mandalay မန္တလေး

Pages 58–59: sunset over Pagan

Preceding pages, clockwise from left: Amarapura; Zeigyo (Central) market, Mandalay; Nagayon Pagoda, Pagan; blue Buddha cave, Eindawya Pagoda, Mandalay; gold workshop; old lady smoking a *cheroot* cigar, Pagan

Opposite: (above) royal palace, Mandalay; (below) sweets stall, Mandalay

Below: Mandalay Division

The resonant name of Mandalay reaches out far beyond the country's borders, with all the associations of its rich and exotic past. This royal city is regarded as Burma's cultural heart, but at the same time it also mirrors the country's movement into the modern age. On the one hand, you find buildings of great historical importance, including the royal palace and the Mahamuni Pagoda, while on the other there is a steady transformation as Mandalay turns into an economic metropolis with a forest of new buildings and a large international airport some distance from its gates.

Mandalay was founded in 1857 by King Mindon, and a year later it replaced Amarapura as the capital. The choice of location was based on a prophecy by the Lord Buddha, who told his disciple Ananda on Mandalay Hill that on the 2,400th jubilee of Buddhism a great metropolis would be built at the foot of the hill. The deeply religious Mindon was a reformer, and under his rule the city enjoyed a cultural and economic golden age. Sadly, though, the era of the mighty Konbaung kings ended soon after his death, when his successor Thibaw was forced to cede Mandalay to the British colonialists in 1885. Together with his notorious wife Supalayat and their children, the last king of Burma was exiled to India, where he died in 1916.

Today Mandalay is especially known for its craft industry. Whole areas of the city are devoted to the production of marionettes and devotional

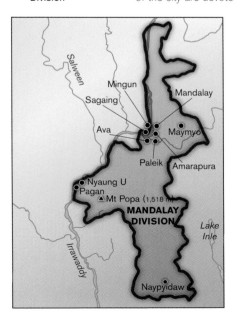

objects made of wood, bronze or marble. You can identify the workshops of the many gold-leaf makers by the rhythm of their hammers as they beat the gold into wafer-thin sheets. Thanks to its accessible location on the Irrawaddy and its proximity to China, Mandalay has become a lively trading centre.

The **Mahamuni Pagoda** in the south-west of the city is one of the three most important shrines in Burma, along with the Shwedagon Pagoda (Rangoon) and the Golden Rock (Kyaiktiyo). King Bodawpaya had it built in 1784, and linked it to his palace in Amarapura by a covered road. The world-famous Mahamuni Buddha, which stands in the centre of the shrine, is 3.8 metres (12.5 ft) high, and over the years pilgrims have covered it with gold leaf, so that some parts of the body are now barely recognizable. In places the layer of gold on this ancient statue is

several centimetres thick and it must weigh several hundred kilograms. Every morning at 4 am, a ceremony is held during which monks wash the face of the most venerated statue in Burma and even brush its teeth. Also worth seeing are six bronze Khmer figures, which are some 800 years old and were originally enshrined at Angkor Wat (Cambodia). Three of these figures are lions, and two are temple guards (*dvarapala*) who, according to folklore, can cure the ills of the faithful if certain parts of their bodies are rubbed. The best-preserved of these statues, however, is a three-headed elephant, the mount of the Hindu god Indra.

Another landmark of the city is the former **royal palace**, an impenetrable complex that was built in 1887 for King Mindon. Covering an area of 4 square kilometres (1.5 mi^2), this is situated right in the centre of Mandalay and stands as a permanent memorial to the final years of the Burmese kingdom. The palace itself, with its many private and public buildings, was made of teak, and during the Second World War was virtually destroyed by fire. The government did not rebuild it until the 1990s, using modern materials, though many people regard this renovation as a bit of a disaster. Another aspect of this renovation leaves a bitter taste: in 1994, 20,000

Above: (left) pilgrims cover the Mahamuni Buddha with gold leaf, Mahamuni Pagoda, Mandalay; (right) Kuthodaw Pagoda, Mandalay

Opposite: (above) Kuthodaw Pagoda; (below) *Tipitaka* marble slab, Kuthodaw Pagoda

citizens of Mandalay were made to clear the moat of mud – a form of forced labour that the junta is all too swift to impose on the people.

From **Mandalay Hill** there is a magnificent panoramic view of the city as well as the Irrawaddy, Mingun and the pagoda-covered hills of Sagaing. Three roofed stairways lead up the 236-metre-high (774-ft) hill, and at frequent intervals there are little shrines and viewing platforms that invite the visitor to stop and marvel. Just before the top, you will come to a standing Buddha whose outstretched arm is pointing towards the palace. This statue alludes to the legend of Mandalay's foundation as being the fulfilment of the Buddha's prophecy.

At the foot of Mandalay Hill lies the **Kuthodaw Pagoda**, completed in 1868. King Mindon employed two hundred craftsmen for seven-and-a-half years to carve out the whole *Pali Canon* in 729 marble slabs – the largest book in the world. Each of these slabs has its own whitewashed stupa, and the main stupa is modelled on the Shwezigon Pagoda in Pagan. In 1871, Mindon convened the Fifth Buddhist Synod in order to consolidate the faith and the unity of Burmese Buddhists. For six months, a team of 2,400 monks recited the complete text of the *Tipitaka*.

The Moustache Brothers
နှုတ်ခမ်းမွေး ညီနောင်

With a *trishaw* one can drive to the 'West End', home to many musicians, dance troupes and marionette artists – and, of course, the internationally renowned Moustache Brothers. Although the name may conjure up images of New York's glamorous theatre district, the reality couldn't be further from the truth. To reach Mandalay's 'Broadway' the driver arduously navigates the bumpy streets, and electricity is only available every two days.

Arriving at the destination, you are greeted personally by Lu Zaw and guided into a small room. Visitors sit on red plastic chairs, and Chinese tea is handed out. The walls are covered with marionettes by Ko Shwe Bo, a nephew of the Moustache Brothers, as well as posters of the opposition leader Aung San Suu Kyi. The *a-nyeint* (the Burmese name for this sort of traditional all-night performance of song and dance) is led by the two moustachioed brothers Par Par Lay and Lu Maw and their clean-shaven cousin Lu Zaw, with wives and sisters of the three completing the troupe.

'My brother Par Par Lay is the boss of our comedy-troupe,' says Lu Maw. 'In the beginning we were three comedians, eight musicians and ten female dancers. For more than thirty years we were travelling from village to village to perform our all-night show. […] We were travelling around to Pagan, Mandalay, Lake Inle, Taunggyi and Pyinmana. Everywhere you could hire us.'

However, in 1996 the situation changed dramatically, as Lu Maw explains: 'On 4 January 1996 our troupe performed in front of the house of the Nobel Peace Prize winner Aung San Suu Kyi in Rangoon. Two thousand people were watching. There were many tourists and members of the NLD. It was a two-hour show with two comedians and eight musicians. Par Par Lay and Lu Zaw made many jokes about the [poor] infrastructure, electricity, education- and health-system, just the daily life in Burma. When they came back from Rangoon to Mandalay by train on 7 January, they were arrested by the military at midnight and sentenced to seven years in prison. I was staying at home in Mandalay to take care of the family and of our house. That's why I didn't get arrested – I could escape.'

Par Par Lay and Lu Zaw were sentenced according to paragraph 5 of the emergency-precaution plan, which states that anyone who knowingly spreads false information can be sentenced to imprisonment for up to five years. This vague, subjective law makes it easy for the junta to control its political enemies. In a camp 40 kilometres (25 mi) away from Myitkyina,

Opposite:
(above left) Par Par Lay; (above right) Lu Maw; (below, from left to right) tourist, Lu Zaw, Lu Maw, tourist and Par Par Lay

the capital of Kachin State, the two were shackled and forced to break
rocks for roads. They were also exposed to malaria, and suffered
malnutrition and exhaustion. The family received no information from the
authorities about their disappearance. After two months of hard labour
Par Par Lay and Lu Zaw were separated and sent to different prisons.
Internationally, the incident caused a huge uproar, and several famous
figures from all over the world – including British comedians Hugh Laurie
and Mark Thomas – wrote letters to the Burmese government demanding
the immediate release of their colleagues. This intervention resulted in the
two captives' early release in 2001.

Since then, public shows by the Moustache Brothers have been forbidden,
and they are only allowed to perform to tourists in their house in Mandalay.
The daily show is a mixture of comedy and traditional dance, reflecting
Burmese legends and culture. Lu Maw acts as a moderator and speaks
in lively English about everyday life in Burma. Risky subjects, such as the
country's widespread corruption, are not excluded. Lu Maw's wife is highly
skilled in Burmese dance and performs various routines for spectators, with
some of her acrobatic moves requiring huge physical strength. Meanwhile, Lu
Maw acts as the translator and explains the meaning of every move of this
complex art form. The traditional music that accompanies the performance
may sound very strange to Western ears. A cacophony of different sounds fills
the room as unfamiliar instruments produce a disharmonious musical display.

At the end of the performance, a police helmet is passed round. This is
the donation box, the family's bread and butter. Paying spectators, and the
inevitable attention they bring, are key to the family, but individual tourists
play another important role, as Lu Maw describes: 'They have more
possibilities to go to [almost] every corner [of the country]. Because

Lu Maw's wife

Above left: one of the sisters of the troupe performing a dance

Above right: the *ogre* character

* Interview with the Moustache Brothers conducted by the authors, Mandalay, February 2006

in Burma one eye is not enough, one ear is not enough. In 1996 and '97 many tourists had taken pictures of forced workers on roads or photographed the cleaning of the Mandalay palace. They made copies for the International Labour Organization, the International Committee of the Red Cross and other non-governmental organizations. That's why the forced labour [has stopped] in downtown areas. Tourists are walking for democracy – they share our feelings. Their protest is different from the other bans. They don't come for the profit – they want to see what's going on here. Because journalists cannot come to Burma, tourists should come and see, like Trojan horses – that's my idea. A democracy means freedom of speech, of writing and worship, an open country, but [Burma] is not [free]. I want the country to be really free. We got an order from Burmese Stasi not to perform, but we don't listen. They say they [will] arrest all our family. Every night we have to [run this] risk. I need the tourists' help."

Until democracy is restored in Burma, the Moustache Brothers will continue to perform to tourists every evening at 8.30 pm in their house in Mandalay, 39th Street, between 80th and 81st Road.

Mingun မင်းကွန်း

Just an hour's boat ride away from Mandalay, along the Irrawaddy, is the little town of Mingun. The public service boats, specially laid on for tourists, leave the Mayanchan Jetty every morning. In this region live the poorest of Mandalay's poor – their tiny shacks stand right by the water's edge, with working animals all around them on the shore, amid the noise and dirt of the ships as they load and unload. Early in the morning, in loud and strident tones, staccato prayers come rasping through loudspeakers, creating a strange though quite impressive scenario for the visitor who is keen to look behind the scenes of the tourist attractions. Even from a distance, one can see from the boat the massive ruins of the **Mantara Gyi Pagoda** (also known as the Mingun Pagoda), which was built by King Bodawpaya to be the biggest pagoda in the world and was originally intended to reach a height of 152 metres (499 ft). For precisely this purpose, between 1790 and his death in 1819, Bodawpaya had thousands of prisoners-of-war and slaves working on the construction of the stupa, but even over this long period of time, only a third of his dream was completed. Twenty years later, the mighty brick edifice was badly damaged in an earthquake. Nevertheless, the remains of the pagoda, 50 metres (164 ft) high and 72 metres (236 ft) wide, are still spectacular. It is possible to climb up it barefoot and from the top there is a magnificent view of the Irrawaddy as far as Mandalay.

Another relic of Bodawpaya's megalomania is the **Mingun Bell**. With a height of 3.7 metres (12 ft) and a diameter of 5 metres (16 ft), it is said to be the largest working bell in the world. The Kremlin bell in Moscow is actually bigger, but it is cracked and therefore not in use. Weighing 90 metric tons, the Mingun Bell was cast in bronze in 1808, and once it was completed Bodawpaya had the master craftsman executed in order to stop him making anything similar.

On the northern edge of Mingun stands the impressive **Hsinbyume Pagoda** (Myatheindan Pagoda), built by King Bagyidaw – a grandson of Bodawpaya – in 1816, in memory of his favourite wife. Its unusual architecture is quite striking. It is based on the Sulamani Pagoda on the peak of the mythical golden mountain of Meru, which is the centre of the universe in Buddhist-Hindu cosmology. Seven terraces with undulating rails – representing the seven mountain ranges around Mount Meru – lead up the stupa, and all the way along are niches in which mythical monsters such as *nats*, *ogres* and *nagas* (mythical serpents, guardians of life energy) stand guard.

Opposite: (above) Mantara Gyi Pagoda, Mingun; (below left) Hsinbyume Pagoda, Mingun; (below right) Mingun Bell, said to be the world's largest working bell

Ava (Inwa) အင်းဝ

With a few brief interruptions, Ava was the capital of the Burmese kingdom for more than four hundred years. No other city in Burma has been the seat of government over such a long period. Founded by the Shan Prince Thadominbya in 1364 on a man-made island between the rivers Irrawaddy and Myitnge, and completely destroyed by the Mon in 1752, Ava lost its status as a royal city several times before it was finally superseded by Amarapura in 1841. Due to an earthquake in 1838, very little remains of the royal buildings. The villages that have now grown up on the site of the former capital radiate an almost idyllic rural atmosphere.

The **Maha Aung Mye Bonzan Monastery**, however, is relatively well preserved. Also known as the Ok Kyaung, this monastery was commissioned by King Bagyidaw's principal wife in 1818, and built of stone in traditional style, with elaborate stucco ornamentations that look like carvings. In the middle of this ochre-coloured monastery is a statue of the Buddha on a plinth, decorated with glass mosaics.

A few kilometres away from Ava, in Paleik, stands the **Yadana Labamuni Hsu-taungpye Pagoda**, also known as the Snake Pagoda, which is believed to have been built by King Alaungsithu in the 12th century. A special feature of this pagoda is the three large pythons nestling at the head and feet of the Buddha, which are said to have appeared in the temple from the nearby forest in the mid-1970s and are carefully washed and fed every morning. Many people visit this place every day to watch the spectacle and to be photographed with one of the pythons. There are countless images of snakes everywhere, alluding to the harmonious relationship between the Buddha, animals and humans.

Left: ancient sculptures at Aung Zaw Pagoda, Ava

Opposite: (above) Maha Aung Mye Bonzan Monastery, Ava; (below) Yadana Labamuni Hsu-taungpye Pagoda, Paleik, known for the three pythons that nestle at the head and feet of the Buddha

Amarapura အမရပူရ

The Sanskrit name Amarapura means 'City of Immortality', although its life as Burma's capital was all too brief. King Bodawpaya initiated the move from Ava in 1783 because he wanted to make a completely fresh start, having acquired the throne through the brutal murder of his rivals and their families. His successors had different ideas, however. In 1823 Ava was restored as the seat of government and, although the throne returned to Amarapura in 1841, in 1857 King Mindon made Mandalay the last capital of the Burmese kings.

The main feature of the charming little town of Amarapura is its many workshops. From practically every house you can hear the clacking of the looms as they produce the most exquisite *longyis* (traditional sarong-style lower garment) of cotton or silk. There are also many bronze foundries and woodcarvers providing devotional objects such as Buddhas and gongs for the lucrative market in nearby Mandalay. All that remains of the former royal palace are the stone ruins – the teak buildings were dismantled and taken away to Mandalay.

Mahagandhayon Monastery, founded in 1914, is one of Amarapura's main sights. This is one of the largest monasteries in Burma, and at times there are more than 3,000 monks living and studying here. At 10.30 every morning hundreds of monks wait in long queues for their meals. At the same time, hordes of tourists stand watching and photographing them, and even in the refectory they cannot escape from the curious and often intrusive gaze of the visitors.

Nearby is the **U Bein Bridge**, which spans Taungthaman Lake, linking the village of that name with Amarapura. It was built between 1849 and 1851 by King Pagan, and at 1.2 kilometres (0.7 mi) is the longest teak bridge in the world. Early in the morning and late in the evening, it provides a popular, atmospheric image for photographers. Pavilions and benches offer visitors the chance to rest, and give the local inhabitants an opportunity to sit and exchange gossip.

Crossing the bridge to Taungthaman village on the other side of the lake will bring you to **Kyauktawgyi Pagoda** (meaning 'Pagoda of the Great Marble Image') which is also worth a visit. This too was built by King Pagan in 1847, and is thought to have been modelled on the Ananda Temple in Pagan. It houses a large figure of the Buddha in bright marble, as well as statues of his eighty-eight pupils. The entrances are decorated with 19th-century wall paintings depicting the signs of the zodiac and scenes from everyday life.

Opposite: (above) U Bein Bridge, linking the village of Taungthaman with Amarapura; (below left) monks at Mahagandhayon Monastery, Amarapura; (below right) Kyauktawgyi Pagoda, Taungthaman

Pagan (Bagan) ပုဂံ

Whichever way you approach Pagan for the first time, whether in leisurely fashion by ship along the Irrawaddy or from the sky by plane, the initial impression will remain indelibly etched in the memory. Across a 40-square-kilometre (15 mi²) area of savannah landscape you will see 2,230 temples and pagodas, their gilded cupolas sparkling in the sun or radiating an almost unearthly beauty in the soft light of morning or evening. Nowhere else in the world will you find a comparable density of sacred buildings in a single setting. It is not for nothing that Pagan is regarded alongside the temple complex of Angkor Wat in Cambodia as one of the most important archaeological and cultural sites in South-East Asia. In 1882, the renowned adventurer Sir James George Scott (Shway Yoe) wrote the following description: '…the whole place is thickly studded with pagodas of all sizes and shapes, and the very ground is so thickly covered with crumbling remnants of vanished shrines, that according to the popular saying you cannot move foot or hand without touching a sacred thing' (*The Burman, His Life and Notions*).

From the Golden Era to the Present Day

When King Anawrahta ascended to the throne in 1044, thereby founding the first Burmese dynasty, Pagan steadily developed into a powerful kingdom (see pages 11–12). By the 12th century the city is believed to have had a population of around half a million, and was one of the most densely populated cities in the medieval world, some fifteen times greater than the City of London. In the 13th century, however, it gradually fell into decline. Financially weakened by expensive building projects and internal quarrels, with provincial governors increasingly unwilling to pay taxes, the Burmese could offer little resistance to the Shan and Mongols who were penetrating ever deeper into Burma. Pagan's fate was sealed in 1287 when the city was overwhelmed by the Mongols and virtually destroyed. Little remains of the Pagan of the past. Palaces and houses have all fallen victim to the ravages of time, and since they were made of wood, all traces have disappeared. Only a few remnants of the old fortifications, including the 9th-century Tharaba Gate, have survived. You will not even find any modern buildings here, because in 1990 the military regime forced all the inhabitants to move 4 kilometres (2.5 mi) away to New Pagan, so that the tourists would have an open view of the pagodas and would be spared the sight of the slum dwellings in between.

Opposite: (above) Pagan's ancient temples and ruins stretch as far as the eye can see, dominated by the impressive Dhammayangyi Temple; (below left) Gubyaukgyi Temple, Wetkyi-in; (below right) Mahabodhi Temple in Pagan – modelled after the famous temple of the same name in Bodh Gaya, India, which marks the spot where the Buddha attained Enlightenment

The best way to see the maximum number of temples is to get yourself a bicycle. There will always be a local guide with a torch to light the way round the interiors and then, in the friendliest possible fashion, to offer you souvenirs.

Among the multitude of pagodas in Pagan, the **Shwezigon Pagoda** is of special note. This was the first to be built in what is now characteristic Burmese style. Construction began under King Anawrahta in 1059, and it was completed in 1090, after his death, by his successor Kyanzittha. Anawrahta wanted to consolidate the Buddhist faith of his subjects, and he brought relics of the Buddha – a frontal bone from Thayekhittaya (Sri Ksetra) and a replica of the Buddha tooth in Kandy (Sri Lanka) – to Pagan, where they were to be housed in a new pagoda. In order to find a suitable location for the stupa, he followed an old tradition: the relics were attached to the back of a white elephant, which was then left to wander freely. The spot where the elephant stopped then became the site for the famous Shwezigon Pagoda. It is now seen as the prototype for all the Burmese pagodas that followed. The basic plan consists of three square terraces with stairways leading up to the bell-shaped *anda*

Above left:
Shwezigon Pagoda, Pagan

Above right:
Kassapa Buddha statue, Ananda Temple, Pagan

The gilded *shikhara* of Ananda Temple

(the main body of the stupa). The tapering rings climbing up the stupa became a typical feature of the Burmese style. On the terraces, green glazed terracotta plaques narrate scenes of the Buddha's past lives, taken from the *Jataka*. With its equal height and breadth of 49 metres (161 ft), the pagoda gives an impression of enormous weight. The *nat* shrine in the southeastern section is well worth seeing – it is the first of its kind in a Buddhist pagoda, where the thirty-seven *nats* are venerated in addition to the Buddha.

At sunset the white **Shwesandaw Pagoda** is hopelessly overcrowded as visitors gather to take advantage of the fantastic view over the temples and the river. This pagoda of the 'golden hair relic' was one of the first to be built by Anawrahta. He is said to have constructed it in 1057, following his successful campaign against Thaton, in order to enshrine a hair relic of the Buddha that had been given to him by the ruler of Pegu. Following an ancient Pyu tradition, the stupa is situated outside the city walls, where along with four other pagodas, including the Shwezigon, it provides spiritual protection for Pagan. Four separate square terraces give the Shwesandaw a pyramidal form, and

formerly there were figures of the Hindu elephant god Ganesha in all four corners.

Perhaps the most impressive of all Pagan's masterpieces is the **Ananda Temple**. It was probably built by King Kyanzittha in around 1090, and according to legend it was meant to commemorate a sacred grotto situated near the mythical Mount Meru. At all four corners of the square base of the temple are porticos that give it the shape of a Greek cross. These porticos lead to passages into the interior, and at the end of these passages are 10-metre-high (33-ft) statues representing the four Buddhas of the present world era. The lower part of the temple is decorated with green terracotta tiles that tell the story of the Buddha's successful resistance against the temptations of the demon Mara and the celebration of the *devas* (benevolent divine beings). The four corners of the *pahto* (temple) are guarded by *manuthiha* lions, which have one head but two bodies. The top of the temple, which soars to a height of 51 metres (167 ft), is crowned by a gilded *shikhara*, on the sides of which are five niches, one above the other, containing representations of the four Buddhas and one of the future Enlightened One, Metteyya (Skt. *Maitreya*).

Opposite: (left) *shikhara* near Mahabodhi Temple; (right) ancient Buddha statue, Gawdawpalin Temple, Pagan

Above: Thatbyinnyu Temple, Pagan's tallest building

The **Thatbyinnyu Temple** is the tallest building in Pagan, rising to 61 metres (200 ft). It was built by King Alaungsithu in the mid-12th century, and its monumental scale helps it to stand out from older temples such as nearby Ananda. Unlike the earlier, single-storey structures, Thatbyinnyu consists of two clearly separate blocks, and it also has two rows of windows, which make it much brighter and airier. There are porticos on both levels at the eastern side only, and in each of these is a figure of the Buddha.

Mount Popa ပုပ္ပါးတောင်ကလပ်

The Sanskrit name for this 1,518-metre-high (4,980-ft) extinct volcano means 'flower', which could not be more appropriate. The fertile earth on the slopes of the mountain and the surrounding plains has produced a large number of rare plants, including orchids, as well as a profusion of trees. The mythical mountain has also traditionally given rise to mysterious tales of strange characters in search of magic herbs.

To the south-west of Mount Popa lies the volcanic peak of Popa Taung Kalat, which is said to be the home of the *nat* spirits and is therefore one of the most important sites of *nat* worship in Burma. A covered stairway leads up the 737-metre-high (2,418-ft) hill, from which there is a fine view over the plain and the whole of Mount Popa. Here you can also get to meet the monkeys that live on the peak and beg for nuts and sweets.

There are life-size figures of all thirty-seven *nats* in a shrine in the pilgrim village, and there are frequent *nat pwes* (ceremonies) held in their honour. The *nats* embody ancestors, legendary characters or spirits of nature, and anyone who dies a sudden death may become one. The particular qualities

of these spirits can be gauged from their dress and the manner in which they are depicted. For instance, Ko Gyi Kyaw is bedecked with whisky bottles because he was a heavy drinker, and it was this vice that took him prematurely to his grave. He is the patron *nat* of tramps and alcoholics, and so it pays them to make sacrifices that will keep him in a good mood. This is the case with all the *nats*, for although they may protect you, they can also do you a lot of damage if you get on the wrong side of them.

Left: whisky bottles adorn this statue of Ko Gyi Kyaw, patron *nat* of tramps and alcoholics

Opposite: the imposing Buddhist monastery on the peak of Popa Taung Kalat, near Pagan

Kachin State

Kachin State ကချင်ပြည်နယ်

Pages 84–85: Mare Hkalup Hpung Church, Myitkyina

Preceding pages: Bhamo; Myitkyina; Mare Hkalup Hpung Church, Myitkyina; (above) San Pawlu Kahtawlik Nawku Jawng Church, near Myitkyina; (below) Kachin Museum, Myitkyina; Myitson

Opposite: St Patrick's Church, Bhamo

Below: Kachin State

Kachin State is Burma's northernmost province, and it is crowned by the country's highest mountain, Hkakabo Razi, which stands at the edge of the Himalayas and towers to a height of 5,889 metres (19,321 ft). There have been many failed attempts to climb it, but in 1996 a Japanese mountaineer finally made it to the top. A trip to Hkakabo Razi is only possible with a state-appointed guide, and it takes visitors weeks on foot, along virtually untrodden paths and through thick jungle, before they catch their first glimpse of the snow-covered foothills of the Himalayas.

Due to the largely poor infrastructure and difficult approach, this is a region that is less frequented by tourists, and yet it boasts some magnificent mountain landscapes and many fascinating natural phenomena, including one of the most exclusive forms of jade in the world which is particularly popular among the Chinese. The belt of rich jade deposits, which runs right through the state, was discovered as long ago as the 13th century and has been exported worldwide since the 18th century. The gigantic mines of the most famous site in Hpakan can only be viewed with a special permit. Tens of thousands come here to try their luck, in the hope of finding a large chunk of the precious stone, and a few have even been successful.

The most visited towns here are Myitkyina and Bhamo, but more adventurous travellers may choose to take a long excursion from Putao in the north, through dense forests. These remote landscapes are home to many different ethnic peoples, some of which are almost completely cut off from the outside world because of the impenetrability of the forests.

The various ethnic groups living in this state are collectively referred to as Kachin, although there is no such thing as the 'people of Kachin'. The most populous ethnic groups are the Jinghpaw, Maru, Lashi, Atsi, Lisu and Rawang, but these are linguistic rather than national distinctions. Indeed, the Lisu and the Rawang vehemently reject the idea that they form part

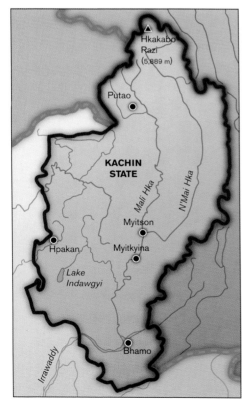

of the Kachin nation. This area is also home to numerous Shan, Chinese, Tibetans and Indians, and owing to its proximity there are a few Kachin ethnic peoples to be found across the border in China too. To the south-west of Kachin State is the land of the Naga, which extends as far as India. This ancient people was made up of a collection of fearsome tribes which long had a reputation for headhunting and resisted British colonial rule for many decades. The Naga, whose traditional culture has remained largely intact, are fighting both in Burma and in India for their independent Naga nation.

The Taron, the last descendants of the only Mongol pygmies, are people living in the inaccessible forest areas of the north; sadly only three surviving siblings are known of, and when they pass away, their bloodline will die with them.

The Manau festivals are one tradition that is shared by the Kachin, and are a particular social highlight. Going back to ancient Kachin animist traditions, there are ten different types of Manau festival, which are celebrated with a great deal of dancing, animal sacrifice, music and alcohol, and can last up to four days. National Day, which falls on 10 January, is a particularly great day in the Kachin calendar, when all the tribal peoples gather to celebrate together on the vast Manau Square in Myitkyina in honour of their creator and most venerated patron spirit Lamu Madai.

Although there are still many followers of the Kachin traditions of animism and *nat* worship, during the British colonial era most Kachin were persuaded by Western missionaries to adopt the Christian faith.

Traditional Kachin house, Myitson

Today 44% are Baptist, 40% Roman Catholic, and just 5% animist and 3% Buddhist. No doubt the main reason for their mass conversion was the Bible. Like the Karen, the Kachin had a 'holy book' of their own that had disappeared, and they saw in the missionaries' Bible the return of their own lost scripture. The first mission centre was built in Bhamo in 1868. Between 1890 and 1892, the Swedish–American missionary Ola Hanson developed the first written form of Jinghpaw, using Roman letters, which gave the Kachin their own script. In 1911 he completed the first translation of the New Testament, and in 1926 that of the complete Bible.

Under British administration, the traditional Kachin feudal system of government continued to hold sway. In the mid-19th century, a revolt broke out against the ruling feudal chiefs (*duwas*), but it was later crushed by the British, who accepted the power of the *duwas*. The British have historically regarded the Kachin as outstanding warriors and during the Second World War sent Kachin soldiers all over the world to fight on different fronts.

From 21 February 1949 on, the Kachin also fought alongside the Karen throughout Burma to gain independence for the Karen, and later they were inspired by the Karen revolution to wage their own fight for freedom. The Kachin Independence Army (KIA) began its struggle in 1961, and its troops rapidly brought large sections of the state under its control. Not until 1994 did the KIA sign a ceasefire with Rangoon to end the hostilities, but the latest political developments in Burma leave this peace treaty unstable.

Myitkyina မြစ်ကြီးနား

Opposite: (above) lavishly decorated Manau posts, built by the Kachin to celebrate their Manau festivals, Myitkyina; (below) the confluence of the Mali Hka and N'Mai Hka rivers at Myitson, where the Irrawaddy River begins its long journey

Below: Richly decorated Kachin bag

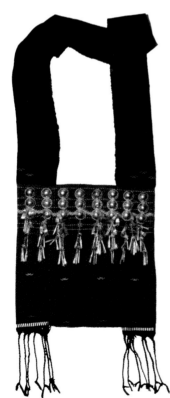

Myitkyina is the capital of Kachin State, and is situated in a picturesque valley 145 metres (476 ft) above sea level. The name itself means 'Near the Great River', and indeed it lies directly on the Irrawaddy.

This lively city has a large food market, and nearby in a stone building all kinds of household goods are on sale, including the famous Kachin bags, which are often decorated with silver. On the banks of the river are a few restaurants that offer a splendid view. A little way from the city centre is the great Manau Square, where in January the Kachin celebrate their National Day with a lavish festival involving traditional costumes, music and animal sacrifices. In the middle of this square are the Manau posts (*manau taing*), which are painted with brightly coloured animals and decorations. Their permanent position in the square is in fact unusual for the Kachin because traditionally such posts have to be destroyed exactly twelve months after the festival.

On the way to the square, you will pass the **Kachin State Cultural Museum**, where you can see displays of traditional costumes and everyday objects, and learn about the culture of the Kachin. As in almost all museums in Burma, however, its collection is fairly meagre, and visitors are unable to get a comprehensive survey of the subject.

Just 40 kilometres (25 mi) north of Myitkyina lies the source of the Irrawaddy, which winds its way through the whole of Burma and is the country's most important lifeline. You can take a taxi to Myitson, which is where the rivers Mali Hka and N'Mai Hka come together to form the Irrawaddy. This triangle is believed to have been the area where the Kachin peoples originally settled. On the banks you can hire longboats for trips down the river, and there are stalls offering drinks and snacks. If you have time to spare and the water level is low enough, you may also go for a walk and come upon gold panners seeking their fortune by the river.

West of Myitkyina, covering an area of 44 square kilometres (17 mi²), is Burma's largest inland lake, the Indawgyi, in the centre of which stands the **Shwe Myitzu Pagoda**. This impressive structure is renowned for its miraculous powers as well as its annual festival.

Bhamo ဗန်းမော်

This little town on the Irrawaddy sees very few tourists, and yet it has quite a lot to offer. Those who do spend a little time here enthuse over the breathtaking landscapes that they encounter on their wanderings.

Bhamo is a trading centre which for many years was an important meeting-point on the way to and from China. Some distance from Bhamo itself lie the ruins of a palace built by the Shan Prince of Sampanago, who once ruled his princedom from here. Sampanago was already known to Europeans as a trading centre as long ago as the 15th century, and today the town still lives on its trade with China and on the sale of rubies. A few years ago, the inner city was destroyed by fire and had to be completely rebuilt.

In Bhamo itself there are a few churches worth seeing, of which perhaps the most interesting is the American Baptist church **St Patrick's**, with its façade of round pebbles. The best way of getting to know the town and its surroundings is by bicycle. Until quite recently, foreigners were only allowed to go a few kilometres beyond the boundaries of Bhamo, but restrictions have now been lifted. You can cycle with or without a guide along fields of swaying rice, past stagnant pools to the ruins of the Shan palace, or to one of the outlying villages.

For attractive landscapes, take a boat ride along the Irrawaddy from Myitkyina to Bhamo and from there to Katha in Sagaing Division. You will sail for several hours through steep rocky gorges and past dense jungle, and by the time you arrive, you will have enjoyed all the splendours of the Kachin landscape.

Below: the traditional Burmese sport of *chinlon*, **Bhamo**

Opposite: rural landscapes around Bhamo

Shan State and Maymyo

Shan State ရှမ်းပြည်နယ်

The former princedoms of Shan today constitute the largest state in Burma, situated in the north-east of the country. Just behind Mandalay rise the first majestic foothills of the Shan Plateau, which can reach a height of over 2,000 metres (6,562 ft). This mountainous landscape is very beautiful, and the mild climate made the region very popular with the British. During the day it is pleasantly warm, but at night the temperatures can drop dramatically due to the altitude.

Another fascinating feature of this area is the number of different ethnic peoples that live in the state. The ethnic majority here is the population of four million Shan, though they actually call themselves *Tai* or *Dai*, the word 'Shan' having been derived by the British from *Siam*. Their close relatives, the Thais, often refer to the Shan as *Tai Yai* ('big Thai'), and the Shan call their land *Muang Tai* rather than Shan State. Like many other ethnic peoples, the Shan were driven out of their home in south and central China by the Tartars, and they migrated to South-East Asia. They settled in Burma, but later the Burmese kings and the Kachin drove them out of the north to the

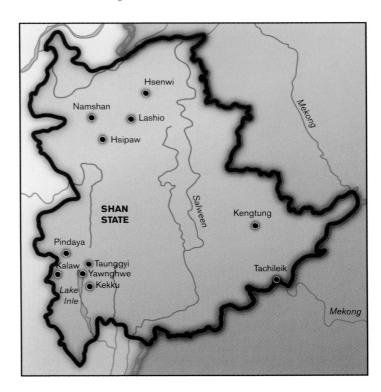

Hsenwi

Namshan

Lashio

Hsipaw

Mekong

SHAN STATE

Salween

Kengtung

Pindaya

Kalaw Taunggyi
Yawnghwe
Kekku

Lake Inle

Tachileik

Mekong

**Shan girl,
Loi Taileng**

northeastern mountains. The Shan also settled in the north of Thailand, the
Hanoi region of Vietnam, India's Assam and the Chinese province of Yunnan.

Until the mid-19th century, the present Shan State was divided into
principalities. The Shan had a feudal system, with princes and princesses
who lived in beautiful teak palaces (*haw*), from which they ruled over
provinces of various sizes. The prince was called *saopha* (in Burmese
sawbwa), which means 'lord of the sky'. He was highly respected by the
people, but if he himself broke the law he could be driven from office.
Like their neighbours the Burmese, the Shan also had a supreme
monarch, the king, and at various points a Shan king even ruled over Pagan.
However, there were frequent conflicts between the rival kingdoms in
Burma. In the mid-15th century, some princes in the lowlands were forced
to accept the authority of the Burmese king, but the Shan peoples in the
eastern plateau were virtually unaffected by this and were able to keep
their traditions.

During British colonial rule, the *saophas* were generally allowed to stay
in power, but between 1922 and 1935 they gradually ceded their authority
to a democratically elected parliament. After the coup of 1962, some of the
princely palaces fell victim to the bulldozers of the military regime, and since
then all traces of their long history have been systematically erased from the

Pa-O women at the market in Khaung Daing, Lake Inle

collective memory. Today, only the Palace of Yawnghwe (Nyaungshwe), a few kilometres north of Lake Inle, is open to the public. The palace in Kengtung, in eastern Shan State, was razed to the ground in 1991.

Together with the Shan, there are a large number of Wa, Pa-O, Palaung, Lisu, Lahu, Akha, Kokang and Intha living in this state. The second largest population is that of the Wa, who belong to the Mon-Khmer people and speak various dialects of the Wa language. An estimated one million Wa live on the Burmese border with China and in China itself. Once they were greatly feared, although they lived in the remote mountains. The British adventurer Sir J. George Scott undertook the first perilous expedition to the Wa region in 1893, and until well into the 1970s the Wa were known to stick human heads on poles in order to improve their harvests.

The Pa-O are a branch of the Karen, and migrated with them from Central Asia. There are about half a million Pa-O now living in Burma, and other members of this people also live in Thailand. They have their own script and language, with six tones. Unfortunately, all their written records are lost, but it is probable that after their migration they established their first kingdom in Thaton, 130 kilometres (81 mi) east of Rangoon. Through many dynasties, they lived alongside the Mon. Following wars with the Burmese, the Pa-O fled north and settled on Lake Inle, where they still live today.

Wa women in traditional dress for a ceremony at the headquarters of the Wa National Army

There are also estimated to be around 100,000 Pa-O living in the region of Thaton, in Mon State. They are easily recognized by their striking costumes – the women's dresses and blouses are black or dark blue with fine, bright-coloured embroidery, and both men and women wear colourful turbans of towelling on their heads. The men's jackets and trousers are also dark blue or black.

The Akha, Lahu and Lisu are smaller ethnic groups who also live in the mountains of the Shan Plateau and speak a Tibeto-Burmese language. The Akha belong to the Lolo people, and there are more clans living in China, northern Thailand, Laos and Vietnam. They have a strong belief in the spirits, have shamans, and build so-called 'spirit gates' outside every village to ward off the demons of the forest. The Lahu and Lisu live in Thailand, Laos and China as well as in Burma, and, like most of the other smaller ethnic groups in Shan State, are for the most part animists.

There are still several revolutionary guerrilla armies in the Shan mountains, who frequently come into violent conflict with the military junta, and for this reason some areas are closed to foreigners. If you want to travel from Lashio towards the Chinese border, you need a special permit from the immigration authorities, and you can only get this in Rangoon, after much discussion and with the exercise of a great deal of patience. Otherwise, Lashio is as far north as a foreigner can go in this state. Similarly Taunggyi, near Lake Inle, is where the door closes to the foreign visitor. From Taunggyi you have to go by plane to Kengtung, the former capital of the principality, as the land route is closed. At the moment, Karenni State (Kayah State), south of Shan State, is totally forbidden territory.

Maymyo (Pyin U Lwin) မြို့

Strictly speaking, Maymyo is not part of Shan State but belongs to Mandalay Division. However, many Shan regard this sleepy little town as their own, because it is situated in the mountains of the Shan Plateau. Its buildings bear the indelible mark of British colonization, and at one crossroads you can still see the **Purcell Tower** – a clocktower that was apparently a gift from Queen Victoria and is said to be a copy of one that she gave to Cape Town in South Africa. The British also established a garrison here, and this is now an elite school to train cadres for the Burmese Army. The town was named after Colonel May, who became its first administrator in 1886. A particularly attractive sight in Maymyo are the colourful horse carriages, which can be used as taxis.

National Kandawgyi Gardens, Maymyo

A trip to the **National Kandawgyi Gardens** makes for an extremely pleasant outing. This botanical garden was built on Lake Kandawgyi by Alex Rodgers with the aid of Lady Cuffle in 1915, using the manpower of 4,000 Turkish prisoners-of-war, and renovated just a few years ago by General Than Shwe. Covering an area of 436 hectares (1,077 acres), the park contains a wide variety of botanical attractions, including a large number of magnificent orchids and bamboo forests, and a rich array of landscapes – from a man-made wetland that visitors can explore via a wooden path, to vast woodland areas that make you feel like you are in the middle of a rainforest. In addition to the seasonal flowerbeds, with their many different colours, you can also marvel at divers species of animals.

A few kilometres south of Maymyo, on the road towards Mandalay, are the breathtakingly beautiful **Anisakan Falls**. A small sign points the way, and after just one-and-a-half kilometres (1 mi) on foot you will come to a bridge where well-trained ladies will guide you free of charge through the rocky gorge and down to the waterfalls. The descent is also stunningly beautiful, but for the return journey you should take plenty of water with you because the path is very steep. Once you get to the waterfalls, you can enjoy the quite extraordinary peace, bathe your feet in the icy water, or watch the wild monkeys doing acrobatics in the treetops.

North of Maymyo stands the **Mahanthtoo Kantha Pagoda**, close to the Pwe Kauk, another waterfall that is less remote than the Anisakan Falls. This is especially popular with visitors during the weekend.

Anisakan Falls, just south of Maymyo

Hsipaw သီပေါ

This dreamy little town is situated on the legendary Burma Road, which the British built in 1940 at terrible financial and human cost in order to create a trade route between India and China. There are still remains of it that one can travel along between Hsipaw and the Chinese border.

The town itself was built in 423 BC, and from 1636 onwards was the seat of a *saopha*. This was also once the home of Inge Sargent, an Austrian woman who became the Shan Princess Thusandi in 1957 following her marriage to the Prince of Hsipaw. The couple were married in the USA in 1953, but it was only when they reached Burma that her husband Sao Kya Seng revealed his royal rank to Sargent (*sao* indicates prince, as opposed to *sai*, which is more or less the equivalent of Mr and of the Burmese *U* in names). They spent eight happy years in Hsipaw and became famous for the social changes that they implemented, which went against the traditional feudal structure of Shan princedoms. Sao Kya Seng was the first prince to give land to the farmers who had been working it for generations and, together with his wife, he also introduced an obstetrics programme which continued for many years after Sargent's flight. It would seem that the generals regarded the Prince as a threat, because after the coup of 1962, Sao Kya Seng vanished without a trace. To this day, his fate remains a mystery, and the Burmese Army continues vehemently to deny that he was ever arrested. There is, however, compelling evidence that this is indeed what happened, and it is likely that he was murdered by the

Stupa at the Mahamyatmuni Pagoda, Hsipaw

Rice fields and houses, near Hsipaw

Military Intelligence. Inge Sargent created her own memorial to the town of Hsipaw with her book *Twilight Over Burma: My Life as a Shan Princess*, in which she tells her own tragic story.

For many years a relative of the Shan Prince known as Mr Donald kept guard over the palace, which was built in 1924. Mr Donald was greatly respected for his courage and feared by the military because of his outspokenness when talking to the tourists who visited the palace. In October 2005, Mr Donald was sentenced to thirteen years' imprisonment for daring to criticize the regime. Today the palace of the royal couple, which stands on a hill at the end of a bridge, is deserted, and a heavy padlock bars the way inside, but Hsipaw continues to be a hotbed of liberal thinkers. On the main road, if you look closely, you will see a weather-beaten sign indicating the office of the NLD, its paint flaking and its rich red colour now faded to a pallid pink.

The surroundings of Hsipaw are very picturesque — a direct invitation for long excursions out into the country. Green fields of rice undulate gently in the morning breeze as the farmers take their oxen to the harvest. The silence is broken only by the splashing of a stream or the whirring of cicadas. If you want to enjoy some peace and quiet away from the tourist centres, Hsipaw is the place to go. There are excursions to the hot springs and to a waterfall, and a few hours away is the Palaung village of Namshan, which was quite recently opened up for foreigners and is famous for its local tea.

Pindaya ပင်းတယ

An hour-and-a-half's drive from Kalaw, in southwestern Shan State, through a landscape of glowing red and yellow somewhat reminiscent of Tuscany, you will come to the cosy little town of Pindaya. From a distance you can see the white covered walkways to the much venerated limestone **Pindaya Caves** winding up the hill like giant snakes. It is possible either to climb the hundreds of steps on foot or take the lift, and once you are at the top you will be greeted by a breathtaking view of the hills opposite and of the town itself, with its artificial lake and the mighty banyan trees around it. According to legend, four princesses were bathing in the nearby Boutalake Lake and were abducted by a giant spider, which kept them imprisoned in the cave. A bold prince killed the monster with a bow and arrow, rescued the princesses, and took the most beautiful of them as his wife.

At the entrance to the dripstone cave is the gilded **Shwe U Min Pagoda**, from which an elaborate network of caves and passages extends deep into the heart of the hill. This houses an astonishing sight. There are over 8,000 gilded statues of the Buddha, in all sizes and poses, made of wood, plaster, bronze and sandstone. Pilgrims and tourists alike stand awestruck before a sea of shining gold, seemingly unable to focus their eyes on any individual statue. Most of the figures were probably made during the 18th century and were brought here by pilgrims. The oldest inscription is dated 1783.

Near the cave one can visit the monastery of **Sein Kaw**, which is named after a stone that is shaped like an elephant. The monastery was built of teak approximately 250 years ago, and it houses various historical Buddhist writings in Burmese, English and Pali, including some *Tipitaka* palm-leaf scripts which are about 500 years old.

Left: statues at the entrance to the Pindaya Caves depict the famous legend of the spider and the prince

Opposite: the Pindaya Caves house thousands of gilded Buddha statues

Lake Inle အင်းလေး

L ake Inle is Burma's second-largest inland lake, 22 kilometres (14 mi) long and 11 kilometres (7 mi) wide. An estimated 100,000 Intha people live on and around the lake. No one knows for sure where they came from, but one theory is that their original home was in southern Burma. In their own language the word *Intha* means 'Sons of the Lake', and their way of life is certainly well adapted to this environment — they live on their fishing and on the produce of their floating gardens. In narrow boats they set out across the water before sunrise, standing with one leg on the stern and using the other leg to row, so that they always have a hand free to scoop fish from the bottom of the lake into their large bamboo nets. This unique way of rowing has made them famous. The Intha have also developed a singular form of aquaculture: a network of interwoven seaweed and hyacinths creates a thick layer of humus over the years, and this is attached to the bottom of the lake with bamboo poles, and then planted with tomatoes, cauliflower, aubergines and flowers.

The tourist centre for those who want to enjoy this wonderful setting is Yawnghwe. Just 5 kilometres (3 mi) north of Lake Inle on the Nan Chaung Canal is the former residence of the last Prince of Yawnghwe and the first President of the Union of Burma, Sao Shwe Thaike. On the night of the military coup he was arrested, and he died later in Insein Prison in Rangoon. The palace where he and his family lived for many years is now a museum. There is, however, no sign to indicate the whereabouts of his grave, which is near the football ground by the canal. After his death his widow, Sao Hearn Hkam, fled to Thailand with their children, and fought for the Shan State until her own death in 2003. The palace itself has retained little of the grace and charm of former times, when princes and princesses would walk across its creaking teak floors. The walls are decorated with dark wooden carvings, and the royal couple's throne still stands in the reception hall. Near the Shan Palace, a little way outside the town, is the **Shwe Yawnghwe Monastery** which is made of teak and incorporates a temple that was built by a Shan prince. The monastery is a regular stopping place for tourist buses, because the young monks standing in the large oval windows are popular with photographers.

Opposite: (above) fisherman on Lake Inle; (below) floating gardens of the Intha people, Lake Inle

Although the town of Yawnghwe is relatively small, it has adapted itself to cater for the floods of tourists that come to the lake every year by building a large number of guesthouses and restaurants. For those with bulging wallets, there are even small hotels on stilts in the middle of the lake, which can only be reached by boat. A whole flotilla of longboats waits on the Nan Chaung Canal to transport tourists to the lake. For a few dollars, they rattle out onto the silent waters in the early morning, bearing their cargo of Western visitors, past the Intha fishermen as they stand on one leg looking for their catch. One of the most popular destinations for the tourist guides is the **floating market of Ywama**, where today instead of food the only wares on show are generally limited to souvenirs for foreigners. Another attraction, and a must for every Inle visitor, is **Nga Hpe Chaung Monastery** ('jumping cat monastery'). Situated on the western shores of the lake, the monastery has indeed become a kind of refuge for cats. The monks take tender loving care of their four-legged friends, and much to the enjoyment of the spectators the cats perform tricks: for a piece of food they jump through rings which the monks hold up high.

At the southern end of the lake is the **Phaung Daw U Pagoda**. There are five statues of the Buddha here, each covered with layer upon layer of gold leaf which has been stuck on as a token of veneration, and so thick is this gilding that the statues are more like balls of gold than images of the Buddha. A highlight on Lake Inle is the full-moon festival of Thadingyut (September/October), which celebrates the Buddha's return from Tavatimsa Heaven and attracts thousands of people from all over the country. Dragon boats race across the lake, and the Buddha statues are carried in solemn procession on a golden barque from one village to the next in order to drive away evil spirits.

West of Phaung Daw U Pagoda, on the arm of a river some distance away from the lake, is the ancient **Indein temple complex**. The site features over a thousand 17th-century stupas, many decorated with fine figures, although some are in an advanced state of decay. Lizards rest in the shade of these weather-beaten, overgrown structures, only adding to the exotic air of the picturesque site. To see all the sights on and around the lake, you will probably need a whole day, because the programme also includes visiting workshops for the manufacture of *cheroot* cigars and woven products.

Opposite: (above) Shwe Yawnghwe Monastery; (below left) Nga Hpe Chaung Monastery has become a refuge for cats; (below right) dilapidated stupa at the Indein temple complex

Taunggyi တောင်ကြီး

Taunggyi was established as a key centre in the 1890s, when Sir J. George Scott had the state's administration moved there, and is the present capital of Shan State. The Western influence is very strong, with the obligatory market and a main street lined with stylish shops. At the end of the main street on the left-hand side, coming from the south, is the plain building of the **Shan State Cultural Museum**, a branch of the museum in Yawnghwe. It does not have a great deal to offer and most of its rooms seem fairly empty, but on the lower floor you can see costumes of Burma's many ethnic groups, and on the upper storey there is a room of Buddha figures.

Once a year, to coincide with the Tazaungmon (October/November) full-moon festival, the famous **hot air balloon festival** is held in Taunggyi. Tens of thousands of people come from all over Burma to watch, as they do on Lake Inle. The Thadingyut and Tazaungmon full-moon festivals are held throughout South-East Asia in honour of the Buddha and commemorate his return from Tavatimsa Heaven, when he was accompanied by a large number of heavenly beings who lit the way for him. The festivals of light, symbolizing these heavenly lights, reach their climax with the long night of the candles at the Tazaungmon full moon, when the monks are given new robes and provisions.

The hot air balloon festival takes place in a square below the **Yat Taw Me Pagoda** ('pagoda of wish fulfilment') and lasts for four days. During the day, schoolchildren and visitors release colourful balloons with animal motifs, which are watched by some very solemn-faced judges who at the end of the festival award a prize for the finest balloon. The balloons are lovingly fashioned from paper, and are lit by burners. For this reason, all foreign visitors are confined to a VIP stand at the side of the square, as the show is not without its dangers. In 2004 a girl was killed by a falling burner. As soon as darkness settles over the town, the balloons – some of which are colossal – are brought to the square and decorated with candles. When the balloon rises into the air, a firework is set off, which fills the night sky with colour.

The balloon ceremony is accompanied by musicians who play and dance to lively traditional Shan music. Every successful flight is greeted by the spectators with wild applause. Meanwhile, along the main street you will find scores of vendors selling food, beer and a lot of trashy souvenirs. Virtually every day there are processions to the festival site, with people bringing precious balloons from all over Shan State or carrying religious tower-like structures laden with alms through the town, to be given to the monks.

Opposite: (above) Yat Taw Me Pagoda towers in the distance; (below) celebrations at the hot air balloon festival

Overleaf: at the festival visitors release hundreds of colourful balloons during the day and light up the sky at night

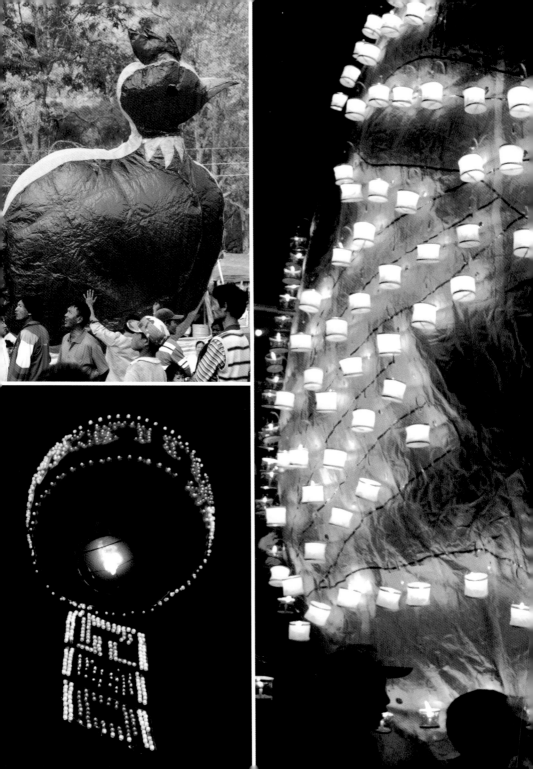

Kekku ကက္ကူ။

The pagoda area of **Kekku** (also known as Kakku) lies just 40 kilometres (25 mi) south of Taunggyi in a region controlled by the Pa-O National Organization (PNO). Since 1991 the PNO has had a ceasefire agreement with the Burmese junta, but for the most part they have retained their weapons. Kekku is the religious centre of the Pa-O people. You can reach the pagodas by various routes, and the employees at the PNO office on the West Circular Road will help you organize a trip and will even arrange a guide for a few dollars. Alternatively, you can hire a taxi without a guide. The drive will last just 40 minutes, and will take you through the homeland of the Pa-O. A much less comfortable route is on foot from Lake Inle through the mountains, which takes several hours.

Kekku itself covers an area of one square kilometre and contains more than 2,500 stupas, which represent the Buddha's footprint. Most of these stupas are thought to date back to the 16th century, although many more have been added over the centuries. Nobody knows the exact origin of this forest of pagodas, but one story is that a wild boar helped a married couple to find gold relics of the Buddha in the ground. As a token of their gratitude for this treasure, they built the first stupa here. Later, the words *wet* (pig) and *ku* (help) were corrupted into the present name *Kekku*. For a long time this temple area was unknown to the outside world, and indeed the Burmese generals pretended it didn't even exist – until a brave German journalist risked life and limb to make the journey and, with the help of Pa-O rebels, became the first foreigner to see the stupas.

Today some of the old, more dilapidated stupas are being renovated, though this is rarely to their advantage. Nevertheless, the sight of these thousands of stupas, tightly packed together and often decorated with legendary, filigree figures, is hugely impressive.

A handful of the 2,500 stupas at Kekku

Karen State ကရင်ပြည်နယ်

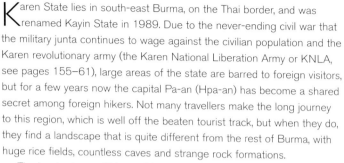

Pages 122–23:
Kyauk Ka Lat
Pagoda, near
Pa-an

**Preceding pages,
clockwise from top
left:** Mount Zwekabin
shrouded in mist;
Buddha reliefs,
Pa-an; religious
mural, Myawaddy;
trishaw, Myawaddy;
a farmer in the
early morning mist,
Kawthoolei

**Opposite: Kawt Gon
Cave, near Pa-an**

Below: Karen State

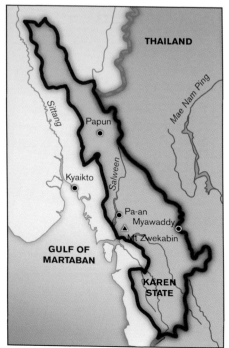

Karen State lies in south-east Burma, on the Thai border, and was renamed Kayin State in 1989. Due to the never-ending civil war that the military junta continues to wage against the civilian population and the Karen revolutionary army (the Karen National Liberation Army or KNLA, see pages 155–61), large areas of the state are barred to foreign visitors, but for a few years now the capital Pa-an (Hpa-an) has become a shared secret among foreign hikers. Not many travellers make the long journey to this region, which is well off the beaten tourist track, but when they do, they find a landscape that is quite different from the rest of Burma, with huge rice fields, countless caves and strange rock formations.

The border town of Myawaddy can only be reached from the Thai town of Mae Sot, as the inland Burmese road is barred. Many foreigners who work in Thailand get their visas extended in Myawaddy, and the place itself has the veritable feel of a border town, with hordes of traders, smugglers, refugees and drug dealers. A great deal of work is being done here on the broad, UN-commissioned Pan-Asian Highway, which is to link Singapore to Istanbul. One stretch of this highway goes through Burma, and its construction has brought about many violations of human rights and the relocation of whole villages without any compensation.

The geography of Karen State is shaped by the Dawna mountain range, which runs right through it, sometimes reaching a height of over 2,000 metres (6,562 ft). The mountains are barely accessible, and very few roads run through the thick jungle. The Karen themselves live in small village communities which are autonomous and are ruled by the village chief. Their lives are generally simple and revolve around agriculture and cattle-breeding.

Like many ethnic groups in Burma, the Karen originated in Mongolia and migrated to what is now Burma during the 7th and 8th centuries. Initially they settled mainly in the Irrawaddy Delta and the present Karen State, but later they were driven back to the Thai border. Even today there are still a lot of Karen in the Irrawaddy Delta, Mon State and Karenni State, although their national identity has tended to merge

with that of the Burmese and the Mon. The name for their own country is *Kawthoolei*, which is a play on words. One translation is 'The Land Burnt Black', i.e. the country that one must fight for (*kaw* = land, *thoo* = black, *lei* = bare), but it is also referred to as the 'Land of Flowers' or 'The Green Land', because the *thoolei* is a common green, orchid-like flower that is frequently to be found in the eastern mountains.

Above: Pa-an landscape

Opposite: Buddha statues at the foot of Mount Zwekabin

The Karen, though consisting of numerous different ethnic groups, are subdivided into the Pwo and the Sgaw Karen, who have developed different languages. The Sgaw are also subdivided into two: the Paku (white Karen), which include the Pa-O and the Kayan (whose women wear metal rings around their necks to make them look longer), and the Bwe, who once again can be split into the Karenni (red Karen) and the Karennet (black Karen). Apart from the various dialects, there are three main Karen languages: Sgaw, Pwo and Bwe.

These differ from Burmese, and research into the original script is being carried out. Once the Karen had their own holy book, the so-called *Book of Life*, which was lost; according to their god Ywa, it would be restored by white brothers sailing from the West. Therefore when missionaries brought the Bible at the end of the 18th century, the Karen thought it was their own long-lost book and thus turned to Christianity. There are, however, still many Buddhists and animists among them. Parts of their history remain unknown because written records have either disappeared or been destroyed.

Pa-an ဟားအံ

Pa-an lies east of Thaton and is a relatively easy bus ride from Rangoon, with the journey taking around eight hours. A more attractive route from a landscape point of view, however, is by ferry from Moulmein (Mawlamyine/Mawlamyaing), which is the capital of Mon State and lies to the south of Pa-an. This four-hour trip takes you up the Salween River to the port of Pa-an. A few years ago, ancient cave paintings and inscriptions were found in the mountains surrounding the city, bearing witness to the fact that the region has been inhabited for many centuries.

This city offers relaxation and the opportunity to explore the magnificent countryside all around, either by taxi or motorbike. The moment you set out along the road to Moulmein, you will be struck by the extraordinary shape of Mount Zwekabin, which the Karen venerate as a symbol of peace. It is more than 1,000 metres (3,281 ft) high, and is difficult to climb, so you will need to take plenty of water with you. However, an early morning hike, when the mists are creeping across the forested slopes, can be richly rewarding. After a few hours' climb, the narrow jungle paths and steep steps will lead you to the summit, from which on a clear day you will have a superb view over the valley. You will also inevitably find wild monkeys waiting for you, expecting you to fill their stomachs with some delicacy or other. At the foot of Mount Zwekabin is a large field containing thousands of over-lifesize statues of the Buddha. A few hundred metres further on you will come to the **Kyauk Ka Lat Pagoda**, situated on a steep rock rising out of a lake. Many writers have compared this place to the scenery of a James Bond film.

Pa-an street scene

Mount Zwekabin

Forty kilometres (25 mi) south-east of Pa-an is Mount Thamanya, where a famous Burmese monk named U Winaya once lived. Aung San Suu Kyi once went on a pilgrimage to this monk, who was known as Thamanya Sayadaw and who established a non-violent zone with a 5-kilometre (3-mi) radius around his mountain. He was a great supporter of the democracy movement and is venerated throughout the country. Every day in his monastery U Winaya used to provide vegetarian meals for 400 monks and 300 female ascetics, and he also built schools for 400 pupils. He died in 2003 at the age of ninety-three.

In former times, Mount Thamanya was known to the Mon as 'Paddy Seed Hill' because it resembled a collection of fields. After the Burmese King Anawrahta had destroyed the capital Thaton, the wife of Thaton's King Manuha sought refuge in a cave in one of the mountains around Pa-an. It is said that later she moved to the foot of Mount Thamanya, where she built the two pagodas that are still there today.

About 26 kilometres (16 mi) away from Pa-an, behind the bridge leading towards Thaton – which is permanently guarded by soldiers who check every vehicle – a track leads across the fields to the sacred cave **Kawt Gon**. Tens of thousands of clay Buddha reliefs have been attached to the natural limestone walls, and the tiled path is lined with statues of the Enlightened One.

Kyaiktiyo ကျိုက်ထီးရိုး

Mon State is bordered by the Andaman Sea in the Gulf of Martaban to the west and Thailand to the east. The first Mon settlers came to this area well over 2,500 years ago and built settlements near the river mouths of the Irrawaddy, Salween and Sittang (Sittoung) in Burma, and the Chao Phraya in Thailand, as well as important harbour towns from which they traded continuously with India and South-East Asia. Coins have been found which show that they even had relations with Rome.

For a long time Mon art and culture were dominant in Burma, and they left a lasting impression. However, the centuries of conflict that followed Anawrahta's annexation of the Mon kingdom in the 11th century took their toll, and with the destruction of their last kingdom in Pegu by King Alaungpaya 700 years later, the independent culture of the Mon finally disappeared. For the most part they have now merged almost indistinguishably with the Burmese.

The Golden Rock of Kyaiktiyo

From their base camp in Kinpun, pilgrims sit jammed together for an hour on the slatted seats of the lorries that take them up the bumpy, winding mountain road. On their way they pass densely forested hills in whose impenetrable jungles the occasional tiger, panther and bear are said to be still living. To get to the longed-for summit, 1,100 metres (3,609 ft) up, the pilgrims must follow a steep path for another hour on foot, or have themselves carried on a palanquin. The stresses and strains of the climb, however, are amply rewarded by a breathtaking panorama of the surrounding mountains and the jungle landscapes, and in the distance you will also catch sight of the main goal of the pilgrimage. Some 10,000 people follow this path every day in order to worship at one of the three holiest shrines in Burma – the **Golden Rock**.

From some vantage points it actually looks as if the rock is about to fall at any moment. According to legend, a single hair of the Buddha is what holds this great gilded boulder in balance. It is said that King Tissa was given the hair by a hermit in the 11th century, who had kept it in his topknot. The king wanted to house it in a pagoda which was to be built on a rock that was shaped exactly like the hermit's head, and when he finally found the right stone at the bottom of the sea with the help of the *nat* king Thagyamin, he miraculously brought it by ship to the top of the mountain, where the boat turned to stone. Ever since

The Golden Rock at Kyaiktiyo, one of Burma's three holiest shrines

then the Buddha's hair has remained in the almost 6-metre-high (20-ft) stupa on the rock.

All around, you will see monks and pilgrims deep in meditation. Only men are allowed to go close to the rock in order to decorate it with gold leaf. The scent of countless joss sticks lies heavy in the air and intensifies the feeling of sanctity that permeates this holy site.

The Hidden Reality

PEOPLE'S DESIRE

- Oppose those relying on external elements, acting as stooges, holding negative views.
- Oppose those trying to jeopardize stability of the State and progress of the nation.
- Oppose foreign nations interfering in internal affairs of the State.
- Crush all internal and external destructive elements as the common enemy.

The Hidden Reality ဖုံးကွယ်နေသောအမှန်တရား

A visit to Burma will produce many highlights of culture and landscape, but the country also has a darker side that may not be immediately apparent. In the shadows of its pagodas, the people are suffering under a brutal dictatorship that has plunged Burma into economic, cultural and spiritual ruin.

In the border regions, a civil war is being waged against the non-Burmese ethnic peoples, who are fighting for freedom and self-determination. Burmese troops continually rape the women of these ethnic minorities, while farmers are arrested at random or even shot without cause as they make their way to the fields. The widespread use of landmines has cost many limbs and lives, and often civilians are used as human mine detectors. In addition, it is far from unusual for children to be trained as soldiers or even press-ganged. Burma has the largest army of children in the world, numbering 70,000. These children have virtually no chance to flee this forced recruitment, and any escape is punished with torture or imprisonment. Most revolutionary armies of the minority ethnic groups, like the Shan State Army-South (SSA-S) and the Karen National Liberation Army (KNLA), send their children to school rather than to the battlefield.

The war against ethnic minorities and the forcible relocation of whole communities has resulted in hundreds of thousands of people being displaced in Burma itself, and three million have reportedly already fled the country into the neighbouring states. The military junta shows no mercy to its political opponents, and any assembly of more than five people can be classed as a demonstration, with severe consequences. Letters are opened and censored, the internet and telephones are constantly monitored, political discussions cannot be held in public, and fear is a permanent companion

Pages 134–35: sifting through rubbish, downtown Rangoon

Preceding pages, clockwise from top left: abandoned rubbish, Rangoon; child soldier of the Pa-O National Army, Kekku; Mandalay Prison; child labour, downtown Mandalay; propaganda billboard, Nyaung U

Left: child labour, Mandalay

Above: transport of female political prisoners at Skekan, Irrawaddy Delta

in all aspects of everyday life. The notorious agents of the Military Intelligence (MI) and paid thugs are nothing if not thorough, and they terrorize the population.

The use of forced labour has a long tradition in Burma, going back to well before the generals decided to 'spruce up' the country in 1996, in preparation for the tourists. However, what they now call 'voluntary work', while improving the country's infrastructure, means that the so-called volunteers can no longer work in their fields, and furthermore they are given no food, accommodation or payment by the authorities for weeks of labour.

The problem of drugs is another running sore. The catastrophic state of the health service, drug abuse and escalating prostitution have led to 360,000 Burmese being infected by HIV according to estimates by UNAIDS in 2005. These figures are on the increase. Only with the aid of foreign organizations, which of course are subject to regulation by the generals, can the country maintain even a minimum of healthcare. A single doctor may have to cope with 19,800 patients, and even more in the border regions according to the United Nations Development Programme (UNDP) in 2000–4. Moreover, Burma also has the worst infant mortality rate in the whole of Asia. According to UNICEF, 104 of every 1,000 children died before the age of five, either from disease or from malnutrition, in 2006.

Burma holds a collection of world records that the visitor will not be aware of: it has the longest-ruling military dictatorship in the world; it has been classified by the World Bank as one of the worst governments in the world; and in 2007 Transparency International also ranked Burma as the most corrupt country in the world.

Opium Poppies ဘိန်းပင်

Accphabet ccording to the UN World Drug Report 2007, Burma has been responsible for the world's largest production of raw opium, methamphetamines and heroin for decades and today ranks second to Afghanistan. Opium has long been a traditional crop in Kachin and Shan States, but it was only through the British that it became important. After they had annexed the Shan States, opium was legalized in 1887 and produced significant income for the colonial administration. For a long time (and often this is still the case) it was the only profitable crop for small farmers, and it was also simpler to produce than rice. There have been times when it was paid for in gold bars, and this gave the most famous opium-growing region its name – the Golden Triangle, formed by Burma, Laos and Thailand.

In 1960, General Ne Win set up a programme for local Ka Kwe Ye (KKY) militias, who were used to fight against the nationalist Shan rebels and the Kuomintang of China (KMT), and in return were given concessions for opium growing and drug dealing. These KKY militias produced the most notorious characters in the Burmese drug business. Khun Sa alias Chang Chi Fu, of Shan and Chinese extraction, became one of the world's most wanted drug barons, and like his rival Lo Hsing Han – a fellow KKY leader – gathered a well-equipped private army around him. Both spent some time in prison, but shortly after his release in 1974 Khun Sa was able to recapture large areas of Shan State. From there his narcotics were smuggled to China or Thailand and then exported all over the world. Publicly Khun Sa always denied that he produced opium and claimed that he was simply paid taxes for providing armed protection to plantations, drug labs and convoys.

The Communist Party of Burma (CPB) and the KMT also used opium to finance their wars. After the CPB had been dissolved in 1989, the United Wa State Army (UWSA) was formed, and when Khun Sa finally laid down his weapons, the UWSA took over much of the drug and methamphetamine trade in its

Opposite: *yaba*
pills, confiscated
by the Shan State
Army-South to be
destroyed

Above: opium fields,
Shan State

own areas. The Burmese Army itself had a long record of involvement in
the drug trade, and collected taxes from it. Even when the government
began an official campaign against the drug trade in 2001, the fields were
often just planted elsewhere, or the destruction of the harvests simply
strengthened the opium monopoly of the armies that were working with
the *Tatmadaw*. Soldiers of the State Peace and Development Council –
the official name of the current military junta – take taxes from the drug
dealers, and in some cases even run factories themselves, producing
the notorious *yaba* pills. Some armed groups such as the UWSA, the
Democratic Karen Buddhist Army (DKBA) – a former rebel group that
is allied to the military junta – and local militias have signed a ceasefire
with the junta, but they too own drug refineries or smuggle their products
across the border and also earn taxes from them.

The ethnic revolutionary armies have strict anti-narcotic rules, and they
attack the factories and drug-runners and burn the materials. They are
genuinely out to destroy Burma's opium fields. The efforts of the Burmese
Army, however, are simply a front; they have no intention of letting such a
lucrative source of income ever dry up.

The Struggle for Freedom

The Struggle for Freedom
လွတ်မြောက်ရေး ကြိုးပမ်းမှု

Pages 142–43: Shan State Army-South soldiers at the 2007 New Year parade

Preceding pages, clockwise from top left: Wa National Army parade at their headquarters; SSA-S soldier, Loi Taileng; 8/8/2006, Brussels; SSA-S soldier on the frontline, looking out over enemy camps, Loi Taileng; monks protesting during the Saffron Revolution, Rangoon, 2007; Karen National Liberation Army soldiers on patrol in the liberated areas of Kawthoolei

During Burma's history, there have been many rebellious uprisings – the current fight for freedom having lasted for more than sixty years. After the immigration of the Mon, Karen, Bamar and Shan, there was a peaceful understanding among the peoples, with a few exceptions, when kings from Lower Burma sent out their troops to collect taxes or gather slaves. However, the Anglo-Burmese wars of the 19th century brought rebellion against the invading British forces and British occupation, and with it arguably the first 'real' battle for Burma's freedom.

A turning-point came in 1930, when intellectuals and students of the Dobama Asiayon ('We Burmans Association') gathered in Rangoon. The members of this organization called themselves *Thakin* (Masters), a sharp dig at the British, who had reserved this title for themselves. Among them was the young Aung San, who was destined to become a national hero. Violent protests occurred throughout the country during this period (1938–39), which were brutally suppressed by the police. This subsequently came to be known as the '1300 Movement', because 1938 was the year 1300 in the Burmese calendar. The *Thakin* movement attracted a large number of Communists, and in 1939 they founded the Communist Party of Burma.

At around the same time Aung San was seeking support from the Japanese to free Burma from colonial occupation. He and his group of twenty-nine comrades – who came to be known as the 'Thirty Comrades' – were trained by the Japanese military and later established the Burma Independence Army (BIA). Together with the Japanese Army, the BIA captured Rangoon in March 1942 and brought an end to the British colonial rule, but they had unwittingly opened the door to the ensuing oppression by the Japanese, who had no interest in an independent Burma. Burmese nationalism was founded in the Anti-Fascist People's Freedom League in 1944, but its roots go back to the British occupation. Many ethnic peoples had allied with the British during the independence wars, and there were several reports of BIA soldiers attacking the ethnic population in revenge for such alliances.

Even after Burma had been liberated from the Japanese with the help of the British, the newly established democracy of the Union of Burma initially stood on very shaky foundations. The Shan, Karen and Kachin immediately demanded their own independence from the Union.

Opposite: mass rally in Frankfurt in support of the uprising in Burma, 6 October 2007

SSA-S soldier on the frontline, Loi Taileng

In order that the non-Burmese ethnic peoples could also have their say in the new formation of Burma's Union, representatives of the Shan, the Chin and the Kachin had met together with Aung San in Panglong (Shan State) in February of that year. On 12 February, all the delegates signed the Panglong Agreement, whereby the non-Burmese ethnic peoples would become partners with equal rights and with a substantial degree of autonomy within the state of Burma. They were also given the option to decide after ten years whether or not they wished to remain within the union, which brought a degree of stability to the country.

In 1948, Burmese troops marched into Karenni State, which triggered a Karenni revolution that has continued to this day through the Karenni National Progressive Party (KNPP). Meanwhile, the Muslim Rohingya in Arakan State, who had suffered years of oppression, also rose up in rebellion. Some members of the Communist Party left parliament and went underground. After discussions for an independent Karen State had broken down, in 1949 the Karen also made a bid for freedom, while the Pa-O and the Mon started their own revolutions. Thus 1949 saw the CPB and several ethnic groups simultaneously taking up armed resistance against the Burmese government.

All these rebellions resulted in the utmost turbulence as the government struggled to get the situation under control. In 1962, General Ne Win

Parade at WNA headquarters

used this political instability to stage a military coup. The students of Rangoon University demanded the immediate restoration of democracy, whereupon the army surrounded the campus, opened fire on the students, and created a bloodbath. The next day, the soldiers blew up the Union Building without even bothering to find out if there was anyone in it. After this, many students went underground or joined one of the revolutionary armies.

In 1963, the government used various strategies to force the ethnic revolutionaries to sign ceasefires. Some did in fact sign the treaties in exchange for concessions connected with the opium trade and the right to control their own territories; these were then left in relative peace by the Burmese government. Other groups, however, such as the Shan, Karen, Kachin, Karenni and Mon, who refused to sign such treaties, felt the full wrath of the military regime. From very early on, the Burmese Army (*Tatmadaw*) was notorious for its brutality and for its savage reprisals against those who resisted it. In the mid-1960s, the junta brought in its so-called 'Four Cuts' policy (*Pya Ley Pya*) to crush resistance once and for all. This consisted of the following: 1) To cut lines of supplying provisions. 2) To cut the line of contact between the masses and the revolutionists. 3) To cut financial sources. 4) To cut the heads off any revolutionaries.

Since then, it has been mainly the civilian population in the ethnic border regions that has suffered under the vicious repression of the government's troops, and any sort of public protest has carried with it a high degree of risk. The country is racked with fear. And yet in spite of the terror, students and opponents of the regime have continued to stage demonstrations, though nearly always with the same bloody result.

SSA-S on patrol through enemy territory

When the junta refused to allow U Thant, former Secretary General of the United Nations, a state funeral in 1974, students and monks again took to the streets to express their anger. Dozens were killed and others ended up in prison or fleeing to the border regions. It was during this period that the National Democratic Front (NDF) was founded, which brought some of the ethnic groups together round the conference table for the first time to form an alliance and then launched joint military operations throughout Burma.

In 1988, the whole country was shaken by the mass demonstrations against the economical mismanagement of the junta, during which thousands of demonstrators were murdered. Following the subsequent coup by the defence minister General Saw Maung there were once again large-

Solidarity protest in Cologne, October 2007

scale arrests to counter further rebellions, and many more students fled to the border regions. In Manerplaw ('Field of Victory'), the former headquarters of the KNLA, they founded the All Burma Students' Democratic Front (ABSDF), which initially received strong support from the KNPP and other ethnic opposition armies.

In 1989 the long-drawn-out Communist campaign came to an end, when the troops and Central Committee of the CPB laid down their arms. This ended decades of civil war, but with their dogmatic ideology the Communists had caused deep rifts between some of the revolutionary ethnic groups. The Burmese troops continued to crack down on villages in the rural areas on the grounds that they were allegedly giving support or shelter to ethnic opposition soldiers.

Meanwhile, more and more opposition groups were gathering in Manerplaw, and in 1990 they came together to form the Democratic Alliance of Burma (DAB) and the National Coalition Government of the Union of Burma (NCGUB) – a government in exile, made up of freely elected members and actually recognized by the EU. Manerplaw thus became the headquarters of the Burmese government in opposition.

When Manerplaw fell into the hands of the Burmese Army in 1995, the various groups had to flee abroad and continue their struggle for Burma's freedom from beyond its frontiers. The revolutionary forces have spread all across the border regions and are now fighting a guerrilla war against the vastly superior Burmese troops, while trying to protect their villages against the army. The government itself, following the tried and trusted British colonial technique, is making every effort to divide the ethnic peoples, promising economic concessions or allowing them to cultivate drugs, in the hope of getting them to sign a ceasefire treaty. They are often allowed to keep their weapons and maintain control over their own regions, but economic support is generally not one of the cards on the table, as the Kachin Independence Organization (KIO) learned after signing their own ceasefire.

The Shan believe that Sanskrit tattoos such as these protect soldiers from harm

Very often the only advantage of a peace treaty is the cessation of military hostilities. Many see it as the only hope of social and political change, and indeed some of the armies actually help the Burmese troops to mount their offensives against other ethnic revolutionaries, or they get involved in the drug trade. Others continue the armed struggle – in particular, the Shan State Army-South, the Karen National Union (KNU) and the Wa National Army (WNA), who took up arms in 1974. The Pa-O, after countless splits, are now with the Pa-O People's Liberation Organization (PPLO) in the midst of their third revolution and are members of the NDF.

In Burma itself, there are frequent spontaneous demonstrations, which are generally crushed with much bloodshed. Former student leaders who have spent years in prison continue to play an active part in the resistance. In September and October 2007, there were escalating protests against the rise in fuel prices, and later the monks led the demonstrations. The so-called 'Saffron Revolution' was the biggest protest for twenty years in Burma, but history only repeated itself, and as in 1988 many people lost their lives or were thrown into prison.

The struggle for Burma's freedom has many faces and is fought on many different levels. There are underground groups that mount poster campaigns and make political demands, whereas armed resistance continues to be the province of the revolutionary ethnic opposition armies, who use guerrilla tactics to attack the Burmese troops and provide defence for the villages in the border regions. Many political activists have fled across the frontiers or to more distant lands, from where they continue to campaign for their country's liberation. On an international level, efforts have been made to impose economic sanctions on the junta and to put pressure on the UN Security Council for worldwide measures, but so far these have been to no avail. It is therefore very difficult to make any predictions concerning Burma's immediate political future.

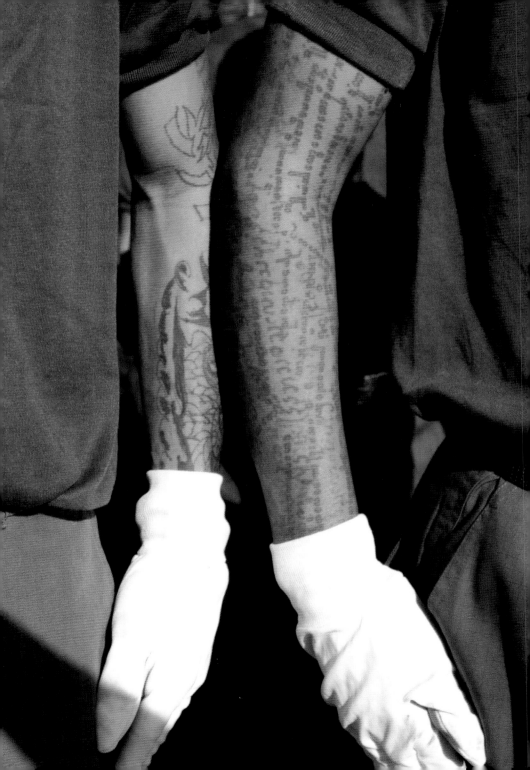

The Karen Revolution
ကရင် တော်လှန်ရေး

Opposite: KNLA soldiers in a newly established camp at the Thai/Burmese border

Above: KNLA badge of the former 7th Brigade

The Karen revolution is one of the longest-lasting civil wars in the world. The Karen are a peace-loving, gentle people and were among the first to settle in present-day Burma. However, after the immigration of the numerically superior Burmese, there were soon bloody conflicts between the two, especially when the Burmese kings began to demand high taxes and slaves from the Karen and other ethnic groups.

Against the background of centuries-old oppression by the Burmese, the Karen revolution is based more on psychological than political grounds, and its purpose is self-preservation. Until colonial rule, the Karen people suffered greatly under the Burmese, and so not surprisingly they sided with the British. The latter, with their policy of divide and rule, encouraged conflict between the ethnic peoples by enlisting mainly Karen and Kachin as soldiers and police.

When the Burma Independence Army freed Burma from British rule, it took brutal revenge on the Karen for supporting the colonizers. Between 1942 and 1945, there were constant attacks, and this calculated oppression has continued under the present government in the form of rape, murder and the destruction of whole villages.

After the liberation of Burma, it was not long before the Karen were demanding their own independence. The reason for this was purely and simply their distrust of the Burmese. Rather than live in constant fear, the Karen wanted the freedom to run their own lives, and on 5 February 1947, the Karen National Union (KNU) was formed under the leadership of the lawyer Saw Ba U Gyi, its aim being to promote a free Karen State. The KNU was in fact a successor to the Karen National Association (KNA) which had been formed as long ago as 1881 to look after the interests of the Karen nation. In July 1947, the first militia was established under the name Karen National Defence Organization (KNDO) and stationed in Sanchaung, a suburb of Rangoon. In the 1970s this was renamed the Karen National Liberation Army (KNLA).

During the turbulent first years of Burma's independence, the central government had little control over its armed forces, and the violent attacks on the Karen people continued. The whole country was plunged into turmoil, with escalating violence against the non-Burmese ethnic peoples. In August 1948, KNDO troops occupied Thaton as well as the important harbour town of Moulmein without a shot being fired. Soon afterwards, Saw Ba U Gyi made the far-sighted political decision to return Moulmein to

the Burmese, in the hope that further military conflict might be avoided and a peaceful solution found to end hostilities. However, the notorious brutality of the BIA did little to aid the peace process. On 24 December 1948, Christian Karen were celebrating Christmas in Palaw, in the district of Mergui (Tenasserim Division), when Burmese soldiers threw hand grenades into the packed church and then, as the churchgoers fled, either shot or bayoneted them. The central government did nothing about the massacre.

Karen soldier in the jungles of Kawthoolei

Shortly after shifting its headquarters from Sanchaung to Insein, a northern suburb of Rangoon, the KNDO militia was banned. Ordinary citizens banded together, disarmed the government troops, and joined the KNDO in order to protect their headquarters. On the morning of 31 January 1949, BIA troops gathered outside Insein in readiness to implement the ban. This was the starting-point of the Karen revolution. The poorly armed Karen held out for 112 days, with little to support them beyond their own will to survive. Further negotiations between Saw Ba U Gyi and the then prime minister Thakin Nu (later U Nu) broke down, and as the position became more and more hopeless, the KNDO troops finally left Insein on 21 May, and the BIA troops marched into the suburb with virtually no opposition. Several thousand soldiers and civilians lost their lives in this conflict.

Hospital of the Karen splinter group DKBA

In 1950 the Karen National Union formulated four simple principles to outline their political position: 1) For us surrender is out of the question. 2) Recognition of the Karen State must be complete. 3) We shall retain our arms. 4) We shall decide our own political destiny. In the same year, Saw Ba U Gyi was shot by BIA soldiers and his body thrown into the sea near Moulmein, in order to prevent the Karen from holding a proper funeral for their first leader and martyr.

The dictator Ne Win opened the gates for another massive offensive against the Karen when he introduced the 'Four Cuts' policy (see page 149) to combat resistance. This operation did not have the desired effect, but it did lead to many more deaths, particularly among the rural population. Karen troops withdrew to the Thai border regions, and were able to receive support from neighbouring states. Their headquarters were then in Manerplaw which was one of the first areas in Burma to be liberated.

In 1992 there were renewed efforts to end the Karen rebellion once and for all. The offensive began with an attack on the strategically important Chweepa Wijo (Sleeping Dog Mountain), which the Burmese troops expected to capture within a month, thus enabling them to march on Manerplaw. In reality it took them three months.

In 1994, a religious rift occurred within the KNU, and the State Peace and Development Council (SPDC) took advantage of the situation to further its own ends. The Buddhist monk U Thuzana wanted to build pagodas in strategic positions, but the KNU leaders opposed the idea because they felt that pagodas represented a security risk. It caused a split of twelve KNU members, and as a result more than 1,000 KNLA soldiers deserted. The junta exploited the dispute to widen the gulf between Buddhist and Christian Karen and thus undermine the KNU, its long-term enemy.

KNLA medic treating Karen civilians

Later, the Burmese General Maung La reorganized the group of deserters and named it the Democratic Karen Buddhist Army, and on 28 February 1995 they joined forces with SPDC troops to attack Manerplaw. The DKBA soldiers' special knowledge of the region was of immense value to the Burmese troops, but a month earlier the KNLA rebels along with various student organizations had already abandoned the hill and burned their headquarters.

Kawthoolei, the Karen name for their land, is hot and inhospitable. There is little or no infrastructure, and the barely accessible Dawna mountain range makes road construction impossible, while agriculture is generally very labour intensive. The one advantage of this hilly region is that the Burmese troops are unable to bring in tanks and heavy artillery. Unfortunately these hills also harbour one of the world's most resistant forms of malaria, which causes immense suffering to the people.

Many parts of Kawthoolei have been designated 'Black Zones' or 'free-fire-zones' by the SPDC, as it is assumed that the villages there are providing the rebels with support. Villagers are at the mercy of the state troops and often are forced to act as porters for the *Tatmadaw*, or to supply them with provisions – which in the light of their own extreme poverty is frequently impossible. They live in simple, temporary settlements, and can barely cultivate enough to feed themselves. Cattle-breeding is generally forbidden. Any resistance to the army's demands, however, is likely to result in an attack that leaves the villages completely destroyed and burned to the ground. Anyone who is unable to escape is immediately shot. When the soldiers have left the village, they mine it in order to prevent the people from returning. Tens of thousands of Karen therefore lead nomadic lives in the jungle, or flee to Thailand.

In March 2006, in an interview with the authors, the 43-year-old headman of an IDP (Internally Displaced Persons) Karen village said: 'The SPDC has already burned down this village numerous times. In 1991 they burned it again and again – two or three times. The villagers moved to Thailand for a while and the SPDC laid mines in the village. The KNLA

troops cannot protect us 100%. If the KNLA receives information about a clash, they come to protect us – otherwise we must escape. But some could not escape and were killed. Just two months ago there were clashes in this village. The SPDC and DKBA troops attacked us last week again and one Karen died.'

Above: Karen children sheltering near KNLA camps

Opposite: IDP refugees on the run

The DKBA, through its special relationship with the SPDC, has been able to construct well-built villages, some of which have a better infrastructure than any others in Burma. It now functions as a link between Burma and Thailand, enabling the country to evade economic sanctions. The DKBA has the right to import used Japanese cars, and it is also heavily involved in the drug trade. Nevertheless, it is beset with internal problems, and its soldiers frequently desert and join the KNLA.

Economic cooperation between Thailand and Burma has made it more difficult for the rebels to obtain arms and ammunition on the Thai black market. For years they have had to wage guerrilla warfare, and a particular weapon has been the landmine. The aim is to cause as much damage as possible to the Burmese troops and thereby weaken their resolve. However, in February 2007 the 7th Brigade of the KNLA, under General

Htay Maung, left the KNU and signed a peace treaty with the SPDC. Their split and the assassination of the long-time KNU chairman Padoh Mahn Sha in February 2008 represented the greatest threat to the KNU since the fall of Manerplaw.

In an interview of March 2006 General Ner Dah, son of the long-serving KNLA General Bo Mya who passed away during Christmas of that year, described the KNLA rebels' task as follows: 'The task of my troops in the area that I control is mainly to protect and survive. We want to make the villages secure and show our strength.'

Shan State Army တပ်ပွဲသိုက်းရှိုင်းတီး

Opposite: (above) frontline SSA-S soldier watches over a camp in the heart of the Shan mountains; (below) flag parade at SSA-S headquarters, Loi Taileng

Above: SSA badges

The Burmese were always somewhat fearful of the mighty princes of the Shan mountains, and so it came as some relief to them when the princes' power was transferred to a parliament. In 1946 the princes established the Council of Shan State Saophas in order to set up a democratic government and divide their power.

Earlier, the British occupation of the Shan States had changed the political situation. The British crown recognized the authority of the Shan *saophas* and so the Shan States, like some other regions in Burma, were given autonomy as a so-called 'frontier area'. The British implemented a few more changes and in 1922 united the principalities under the umbrella of the Federated Shan States. Under British guidance, a central government was formed (Shan State Council), consisting of the thirty-three princes of the individual states and the British representatives.

After Burma had been liberated from the British and the Japanese, the Shan princes took their place in the newly elected parliament, but it was not clear whether the state should form part of the new Union of Burma. On 7 February 1947 the little town of Panglong witnessed the first raising of the Shan national flag, and the national anthem received its first official performance. The first democratically elected Shan State Council consisted of seven citizens and seven representatives of the princes. The Council demanded autonomous administration and subsequent separation from the Burmese state once independence had been achieved.

This autonomy was guaranteed by the legendary Panglong Agreement, which was signed on 12 February 1947 and gave the Shan and other nations the right to decide after ten years whether or not they wished to remain part of Burma or to set up their own independent state. The Shan trusted General Aung San and the Burmese, and joined the Kachin and the Chin in signing the treaty, but with the murder of Aung San, the promise of independence also died, and all the efforts of the princes to find a political solution to the problem foundered.

When the Chinese Kuomintang marched into Shan State and occupied large sections of it in 1950, Burmese troops also invaded – in order to fight the Chinese – and so the Shan themselves saw their country being occupied by two foreign armies, at whose hands they experienced nothing but suffering. In 1958 a group of students went into the jungle near the Thai border and founded the Noom Suk Harn ('Brave Young Warriors') – the first national liberation army of the Shan.

After the ten-year period stipulated in the Panglong Agreement had elapsed, it became clear that there was no chance of the Shan being allowed to fulfil their dream of self-determination. In 1960, students formed the Shan State Independence Army (SSIA) which allied two years later with the Noom Suk Harn to form the Shan National United Front (SNUF) as a forum to unite the Shan national forces. During the night of Ne Win's coup, members of the Shan Parliament were arrested, including the former President of Burma and Prince of Yawnghwe, Sao Shwe Thaike. His wife Princess Sao Hearn Hkam was instrumental in the foundation of the Shan State Army (SSA), which was established on 22 April 1964 in the Thai town of Chiang Mai (when the SSIA and SNUF joined forces) and through the Shan State Army-South is the main force in the present Shan rebellion. She became head of the war council, which dealt with political matters and with contacts abroad, and her son Tzang Yawnghwe fought as a commander for many years before quitting the army in 1976 and fleeing to Thailand. Later he flew to his mother in Canada, where he passed away in 2004. Sao Hearn Hkam died in 2003 at the age of eighty-six.

The never-ending conflict between the Kuomintang, the armies of the Communist Party and the *Tatmadaw* ravaged the whole of Shan State, and the people suffered appallingly. In addition, the many local militias and the

SSA-S parade, Loi Taileng

SSA-S women's brigade, Loi Taileng

armies of the drug-lords were also continually at war with one another or with the national Shan revolutionaries. All of these armies plundered, exploited or killed the ordinary people to further their own ends, bringing misery and extreme poverty to the remote hills of the Shan Plateau.

The Burmese troops' implementation of the 'Four Cuts' policy, which was directed against all ethnic groups in arms, caused further havoc, and the very presence of these soldiers emphasized the manner in which the Shan people had been betrayed: instead of the promised autonomy, they now found themselves once more under foreign occupation. As in Karen State, whole villages are still being relocated, and farmers are made to do forced labour or to act as porters during military operations. A particularly shocking report on the practice of mass rape by Burmese soldiers – *Licence to Rape* – was published in 2002 by the Shan Women's Action Network (SWAN).

The present Shan State Army is composed of many different resistance organizations. In 1984 the Shan United Revolutionary Army (SURA), led by General Gawnzerng (Moh Heng), joined with the Shan United Army (SUA) of the drug baron Khun Sa to form a new Shan State Army, which was renamed the Muang Tai Army (MTA, meaning 'Shan State Army') in 1987. Gawnzerng was vehemently opposed to the cultivation and trade of opium, and espoused the policies of the SSA, which had publicly denounced the

trade since 1971, and hence cooperation with Khun Sa and his SUA was a highly ambivalent process. There was no getting away from the fact that Khun Sa was a prosperous businessman who had made his fortune through drugs, although he insisted that he had always fought for the freedom of his people and needed opium to finance the struggle. The invasion by Burmese, Chinese and Communist forces had reduced the Shan State to abject poverty, and so in his opinion opium was the farmers' only chance of making any sort of living.

In 1996, Khun Sa finally surrendered to Rangoon, but many members of the MTA then left and joined with soldiers from the SURA to re-establish the Shan State Army. The word 'South' was added in order to distinguish it from the SSA in the north, which also signed a ceasefire treaty. There followed a meeting with representatives of the civilian population to decide whether the SSA-S should fight on. The Shan people voted against a ceasefire and in favour of continuing the struggle for self-determination. Since 1996 the commander of the SSA-S has been the charismatic Colonel Yawd Serk. Various media campaigns by the SSA-S have resulted in Yawd Serk being featured on the front pages of Thai newspapers, and the Shan movement is

Above left: Colonel Yawd Serk

Above right: SSA-S soldiers in formation

now well known among the Thai people. The close cultural ties and shared memories of their own conflicts with Burma have left many Thais sympathetic to the Shan cause, and several music albums, books and films about Yawd Serk and the SSA-S have already appeared in Thailand.

Gawnzerng was also responsible for setting up the Tai Revolutionary Army (TRA) and its political body the Tai Revolutionary Council (TRC), of which he was the chairman until his death in 1991. Since 1999, the TRC has been renamed the Restoration Council of the Shan State (RCSS) and constitutes the political and civilian arm of the SSA-S. Its base is in Loi Taileng, a small, well-organized town that was built after the break-up of the MTA and is also the headquarters of the SSA-S. The RCSS has 300 members and twenty-one elected representatives who meet twice a year. Its aim is to bring about unity – with or without a ceasefire – between the warring rebel ethnic groups, in order to fight together for a free Shan State. According to the political manifesto of the RCSS, *The Four Noble Principles & Six Objectives* (1999): 'All these ethnic groups have birth and live, together for generations, help each other in need and all had participated in protecting our homeland. So, all these ethnic groups should include in our nation [*sic*].'

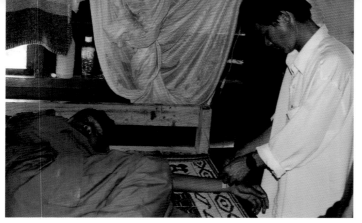

Left: medical treatment, SSA-S clinic

Opposite: (above) orphans and children of refugees queue for their lunch; (below) IDP refugees take shelter near SSA-S headquarters, Loi Taileng

The many years of war have resulted in a large number of Shan now being constantly on the move. Some of them find refuge in the camps of the SSA-S, and are thus able to escape from the rape and brutality of the Burmese troops, as described by Ow Fan Na in an interview with the authors (Loi Taileng, November 2006): 'Over three years [we had to do forced labour]. A long time. We didn't have time to farm or to plant for ourselves. I had already planted the rice in the upland, but I didn't have time to harvest [it]. Very difficult. I had to start to move to another place and so I decided [with my family] to come here [Loi Taileng]. Just before midnight we gathered some of our belongings and left our village. The next day an SPDC troop came to our village and asked: "Where is this family?" "Gone!"'

With the arrival of the refugees, the SSA-S built schools and hospitals, and took care of the many orphans who had lost their parents in the fighting. But they have very few resources, and can cater only for the bare necessities of the refugees. The Shan have no refugee camps in Thailand, unlike the Karen and the Karenni (owing to their close cultural ties with the Thai people). Instead, many Shan live illegally in Thailand, which creates a whole new set of problems.

The Shan State Army has long sought to find a political solution, but so far without success. All of the RCSS's proposals have been rejected by the National Convention, particularly since the Shan insist on the implementation of the all-important Panglong Agreement of 1947. Meanwhile, their troops continue to protect the people against the attacks of enemy soldiers and to grapple with the drug problem that is so destructive both of the state and of its people. The SSA-S has revived its anti-narcotics policy since 1996 and is waging war on drugs, although it receives no support from any organized body. Its troops patrol the whole state and launch raids on drug factories as well as stopping couriers who try to cross the border.

8.8.88 ၈၈၈၈

The terrible day in August 1988, and the nightmare weeks that followed, have entered into the darkest pages of Burma's history, in their way anticipating the similar atrocities that took place during the Tiananmen Square protests in Beijing the following year. But there were no foreign cameras present in Burma, and so the massacre attracted little international attention.

The run-up to these events lay in the ever-worsening state of the country's economy, which drove the people out onto the streets in an effort to end decades of economic incompetence by the military dictators. On 5 September 1987, the government declared that all 25, 35 and 75 kyat banknotes were invalid but no compensation would be paid. Many Burmese have no confidence in the banks and so had kept their savings at home, and in the space of a day they became bankrupt. In the months that followed, there were strikes and student demonstrations, joined by more and more people. During a fist-fight between students and citizens in a teashop in a Rangoon suburb, a student was badly injured but the culprit was later released by the police. The next day, this injustice led to another demonstration, which was crushed by the dreaded Lon Htein riot police, with 200 students being arrested and one – Maung Phone Maw – shot dead. Six or seven other students later died from their gunshot wounds. These were the first victims in a series of massacres that took place during subsequent demonstrations. Burmese in exile still commemorate this day on 13 March 1988 as Burma Human Rights Day.

Three days after this incident, another demonstration by several student groups near Lake Inya was blocked by the Lon Htein and the military. Many students were killed and drowned in the lake. The White Bridge, where this horror story took place, ran red with students' blood. Between May and July there were many such attacks, which spread terror throughout the population, but the demonstrations went on, with the protesters often using home-made weapons such as jinglees (darts or arrows made from spokes), slingshots, swords and crossbows to defend themselves against the vicious attacks of the soldiers and riot police. On 1 July the government imposed a curfew from 8 pm till 4 am, with the following warning: '…if in future there are mob disturbances, if the army shoots, it hits – there is no firing in the air to scare' (Bertil Lintner, *Outrage: Burma's Struggle for Democracy*, 1990). The curfew deprived many of the smaller shops of their income, as most people had to leave home very early in order to get to work. Then suddenly,

Mass rallies in Rangoon, August 1988

to everyone's surprise, General Ne Win officially resigned, and Sein Lwin took over his duties on 25 July 1988, although it soon became clear that Ne Win remained the driving force behind the government.

At the beginning of August, the All Burma Students' League distributed leaflets calling for a general strike on 8 August. This date had been chosen by astrologers, and was reminiscent of the 1300 Movement in 1938. At 8.08 am on the appointed day, the dockworkers left the docks to join other columns of demonstrators who were heading from all directions towards the centre of Rangoon. Students, women, monks, children and even some government employees came together in their hundreds of thousands to protest against the government's mismanagement of the economy and to demand an end to the totalitarian regime. The streets echoed with the people's cries for freedom and justice. As the day neared its end, there was euphoria in the air because the soldiers had done nothing to stop the demonstrations.

But the night was not yet over. In his book *Outrage: Burma's Struggle for Democracy*, Bertil Lintner writes this account: 'At 11 pm there were still thousands of people outside the Sule Pagoda. At 11.30, trucks loaded with troops roared out from behind the City Hall. These were followed by more trucks as well as Bren-carriers, their machine-guns pointed straight in front of them. Spontaneously, the demonstrators began singing the national anthem. Two pistol shots rang out – and then the sound of machine-gun fire reverberated in the dark between the buildings surrounding Bandoola Square. People fell in droves as they were hit. The streets turned red with blood as people "scattered screaming into alleys and doorways, stumbling over open gutters, crouching by walls and then, in a new wave of panic, running again", Seth Mydans wrote in the *New York Times* of 11th August.'

During the weeks that followed, all eyes were on Sein Lwin, whom the Burmese referred to as 'The Butcher' from then on. There were mass demonstrations all over the country, with government soldiers invariably firing at random into the crowds. Reports from Mandalay, such as this one by the Kayan author Pascal Khoo Thwe (in *From the Land of Green Ghosts*, 2002), were just like those from Rangoon: 'Monks and students now led the growing demonstrations in Mandalay. In the neighbouring town of Sagaing, many demonstrators were shot dead and their corpses dumped into the Irrawaddy and into sandpits. When rumours of this reached me I was unable to believe them. [...] I took my bicycle and rode down to Sagaing, and dismounted beneath the Sagaing bridge. As I stood there, I saw twenty or thirty corpses float past. I still do not understand why the regime made no attempt to hide the evidence of the atrocities – unless it was terror or express contempt.'

Protesters commemorate 8.8.88 outside the Burmese embassy in Brussels, 8 August 2006

More than 10,000 people lost their lives. From 8 August until 3 October 1988 the whole country was rocked by civil war, with demonstrations taking place daily and running street battles between the police, soldiers and demonstrators. While all this was going on, the governing Burma Socialist Programme Party (BSPP) held an emergency meeting, because all foreign exchange transactions had been frozen in protest against the massacres. Shortly afterwards, the BSPP was disbanded, thus putting an end to the Burmese version of Socialism. The new rulers called themselves the SLORC (now the SPDC) and promised free elections, and so the riots of 1988 died down, with renewed hope for democracy. But Burma was rife with rumours that the riots of 8.8.88 had actually been planned by General Ne Win. He had realized that his Burmese (pseudo-)Socialism was not working. It was said that he had used the demonetization of kyat notes in 1987 and the resultant unrest in 1988 to withdraw from the political stage so that he could go on pulling the strings from behind the scenes and disband the BSPP.

On 8 August every year, all over the world, exiled Burmese gather outside the government's foreign embassies to commemorate the victims of those dark weeks.

Aung San Suu Kyi အောင်ဆန်းစုကြည်

Aung San Suu Kyi is undoubtedly the best-known figure in the Burmese democratic movement. In Burma her name is mentioned only in hushed tones when no one else is listening, and indeed many refer to her simply as 'The Lady'. She was born on 19 June 1945 in Rangoon, daughter of General Aung San and Daw Khin Kyi. When her father was murdered in 1947, she was just two years old. She studied at Oxford, where she met the English Tibetologist Michael Aris. Later they were married and had two children, Alexander and Kim. When her mother Daw Khin Kyi fell seriously ill, Aung San Suu Kyi travelled to Rangoon in March 1988 in order to be with her as she lay dying. At this time, the country was reeling under the impact of mass demonstrations, which despite her own private grief could hardly fail to have had an effect on her. As the daughter of the Burmese national hero Aung San, who had led his country to independence, she felt compelled to raise her own voice in protest against the military dictators.

On 26 August 1988 she made her second public speech at the foot of the Shwedagon Pagoda. Hundreds of thousands of people came to hear her, eager to listen to what she had to say. Her message was loud and clear: 'I could not as my father's daughter remain indifferent to all that was going on. This national crisis could in fact be called the second struggle for national independence' (*Freedom from Fear*, 1995). Those present cheered long and loud, and over the next few months Aung San Suu Kyi became a key figure in the new resistance for democratic change. Her charisma and her strength gave renewed courage to many of her fellow countrymen.

By advocating non-violent resistance in the form of civil disobedience, she followed the path laid down by Mahatma Gandhi and Nelson Mandela. Along with other democratic opponents of the regime, she founded the National League for Democracy in September 1988, and became its General Secretary. She then spent several months travelling around the country, and thousands came to listen to her. On 20 July 1989, the junta put her under house arrest for the first time. The popular support that she and the NLD were getting represented a real danger to the military, and even today, despite an overwhelming election victory in 1990 with 82% of seats, Aung San Suu Kyi and her party are still called the opposition and are the subject of vehement defamation.

For her continued resistance and her indomitable will in defying all the odds to fight for her people, she was awarded the Sakharov Prize for

Aung San Suu Kyi
on a visit to the
Moustache Brothers,
2003

Freedom of Thought in 1990 and the Nobel Peace Prize in 1991 – these to go with countless other honours. But Aung San Suu Kyi still remains isolated from the outside world, forced to live alone in her house at 54 University Avenue on Lake Inya. You would be well advised to stay away from the house, because the street is sealed with military barricades, and no foreigner is allowed to enter. Her telephone is cut off, and she is not allowed to leave the house or receive visitors. When her husband fell ill with cancer, he was refused a visa, and so she never saw him again. He passed away in 1999. From time to time her house arrest has been lifted, and on one of the last occasions, in 2003, she narrowly escaped assassination. The would-be killers were bandits hired by the Military Intelligence.

Altogether Aung San Suu Kyi has now (October 2008) been confined for twelve years, and despite continued pressure from the international community, there appears to be no end in sight to this isolation. The last public glimpse of her was during the demonstrations by the monks in September 2007.

The Saffron Revolution
ရွှေ၀ါရောင် တော်လှန်ရေး

In 2007 Burma once again hit the international headlines when soldiers opened fire on peacefully demonstrating monks and other civilians. In February some fifty people took to the streets in Rangoon to protest against the military junta. There were a few arrests, and the demonstrations more or less fizzled out. Then on 14 August the government announced a 500% increase in the price of fuel, and within a week the people began to vent their frustration at the ever-rising rate of inflation and the junta's continued mismanagement of the economy. On 21 August several hundred marched in protest but were soon forced off the streets and taken away in buses. The next day, more than 500 people from different townships in Rangoon took to the streets, and were attacked with iron bars and machetes by members of the Union Solidarity and Development Association (USDA), a government-sponsored organization. During the next few days, the protest movement spread like wildfire, and more and more people came out to demonstrate despite the continued repression, but the dark clouds were already gathering as military units began to head for Rangoon.

The situation escalated very rapidly on 5 September when the first monks appeared on the streets of Pakokku, a little town near Pagan. The 600 monks and 10,000 spectators were stopped by soldiers firing warning shots over their heads, but in response the monks later set fire to the cars of government officials, called for a boycott of alms given by the military and their families, and demanded an apology for what had happened.

On 21 September, Rangoon saw monks take to the street in their first mass protest. Several hundred streamed into the centre of the city, praying and chanting their Buddhist psalms, and were cheered on by the people, who formed human chains to protect the protest from military attack. The security forces, however, held back. The following day saw hundreds more monks join the protest, and on their way from the Shwedagon Pagoda they even dared to pass by the house of Aung San Suu Kyi. In tears, she stepped out of her house for a moment to greet the monks. Over the next few days, the crowds of demonstrators continued to grow, as thousands of monks and hundreds of thousands of civilians marched through the streets, watched by thousands more who were cheering from their windows and balconies. The mood of rebellion had now spread to other towns all over Burma.

On the evening of 25 September, the security forces – which had long been waiting in the wings but had continued to hold back – finally reacted. A curfew was imposed, and the police were given heavy reinforcements.

Revolution in Rangoon: (opposite, above left) a monk raises his upside-down alms bowl, a sign of disrespect aimed at the military; (above right) injured protester; (below) civilians form a protective chain around the monks in support

When the monks tried to assemble the next morning at the Shwedagon
Pagoda, they were driven back with teargas and batons. The same day
witnessed the first deaths in Rangoon, as the soldiers opened fire. The
exact number of people killed during the protests is still unknown, but the
opposition estimates that it ran into hundreds. The official figure was fifteen.

On 27 September, monasteries all over Burma were surrounded by
soldiers, so that the monks were unable to take part in any demonstrations.
Large numbers were arrested and abused. In the meantime, police and
soldiers cracked down on the civilian demonstrators, who had gathered
in their thousands, shooting at random into the crowds. Hundreds were
arrested, and many died in the hail of bullets. Japanese journalist Kenji
Nagai was one of those hit and later died in hospital in Rangoon. Over
the next few days, faced with the brutality of the security forces, the
demonstrators vanished as swiftly as they had come. More than 3,000
people were thrown into prison, and many disappeared without trace.

The savage conduct of the police and soldiers caused an international
outcry, and hundreds of thousands of people took part in demonstrations
of solidarity all over the world. The USA and EU imposed stricter sanctions

**Protesters take
to the streets in
Rangoon during the
Saffron Revolution
in September 2007
(above) and in
Frankfurt on 6
October 2007
(opposite)**

on Burma, and a UN envoy, Ibrahim Gambari, travelled round the seething country and tried to mediate between the junta and Aung San Suu Kyi. A minister was appointed to lead future discussions with the opposition, but meanwhile the SPDC staged nationwide demonstrations in support of the National Convention, as an attempt to improve its image. Months after the September protests, people were still being arrested, and the junta refused to hold any meaningful talks with opposition leaders or ethnic groups.

The events of September 2007 constituted the biggest protest movement since 1988. The harsh measures taken by the government brought back all the bitter memories both at home and abroad of the massacres that had taken place nineteen years earlier. Thanks to the internet, the media worldwide were able to broadcast daily reports on events as they happened, and for a short time the international community focused its attention on the problems that have tormented the Burmese for so long.

The spirit of rebellion is still very much alive, and the younger generation especially has been inspired by the communal solidarity of those days. The torch has been lit, and the burning desire for freedom, self-determination and democracy is not so easily extinguished.

Burma in Exile

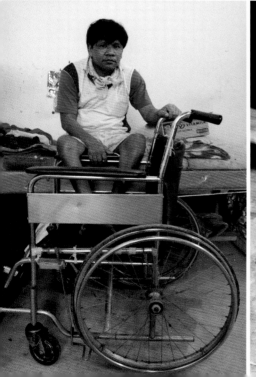

Refugees ဒုက္ခသည်

Pages 182–83:
ill and disabled
Burmese children
and orphans,
sheltering in homes
run by the Social
Action for Women,
Mae Sot, Thailand

Preceding pages,
clockwise from top
left: Mae La refugee
camp, near Mae
Sot, Thailand;
demonstration to
commemorate the
Depayin massacre of
2003, Brussels, 2007;
refugee children in
the Mae La camp;
the Mae Tao clinic
in Mae Sot provides
refugees with
medical care,
wheelchairs and
prostheses; Kayan
woman in her
makeshift home in
the Ban Mai Sai Noi
camp, near Mae
Hongson, Thailand

Due to the Burmese Army's flagrant violations of human rights and continued repression of the civilian population, it is estimated that around 540,000 people are permanently on the move within the country itself. Some of these Internally Displaced Persons (IDPs) are hiding in the jungle and shift from one place to another, according to the state of battle, while others have been forcibly relocated by the government into temporary settlements where they are more easily kept under surveillance. There are also many IDP villages in the areas liberated by the ethnic resistance as well as in those where the rebel groups have signed a truce with the junta. What all of them have in common is a total lack of security, with the knowledge that their lives may be radically changed from one day to the next. Above all, it is the refugees who have fled to the 'Black Zones' (or 'free-fire zones') who are constantly exposed to the danger of attack by government forces; they have no fixed accommodation of any kind but must be prepared to flee at any moment. Their former homes have been destroyed by the *Tatmadaw* and the means by which they may have earned a living – such as crops or animals – have been stolen or burned. Thousands of people have already been maimed, raped, sent to do forced labour or killed.

The civil war and the appalling living conditions have also resulted in some three million people seeking refuge in neighbouring countries. Bangladesh has officially taken in about 20,000 Rohingya who are housed in two refugee camps, but it is estimated that around 200,000 have entered the country illegally. More than 50,000 Chin and Kachin have fled to the northeastern states of India but are not recognized as refugees by the Indian government and therefore receive no aid or support. At least 40,000 Burmese are living in Malaysia – mainly Rohingya and Chin – and although the Malaysian government has promised them temporary residence permits, they live in constant danger of being arrested by the immigration authorities and deported.

The largest number of Burmese refugees are living in Thailand. More than 150,000 of them – mainly Karen and Karenni – are housed in nine refugee camps along the Burmese border, where they are looked after by various international aid organizations and the UN High Commissioner for Refugees. The largest camp, in Mae La, contains more than 45,000 people, living in extremely cramped conditions. Many of them fled to Thailand some twenty years ago, and the younger generation was born in the camps and has no first-hand knowledge of the homeland. 'I left my parents when I was

Opposite: inside
the Mae La refugee
camp

13', says a Karenni youth, Lu Pee (interview with the authors, Mae Hongson, November 2006). 'Our village was relocated by the SPDC, and so was another village close by. We heard rumours that the soldiers were forcing children to join the army. I didn't want to be a soldier, so I ran away to Thailand.'

Refugees must obtain a permit before they are allowed to leave their camp, and they cannot look for work anywhere else. Many of them, however, risk being caught by the Thai police and go to work in nearby factories in order to supplement the basics that are provided in the camps. The USA and other Western nations such as Canada and Australia have been accepting some of these refugees since 2005, but first the applicants must pass through a strict selection procedure to prove that they have not given any form of support to a military organization. Even forced labour for the *Tatmadaw* or giving provisions to soldiers of the ethnic liberation armies constitutes grounds for rejection. Sometimes families are torn apart by these procedures if some members fail to pass the test. Another critical factor in this policy of resettlement is the 'brain drain', because for the most part it is young and relatively well-educated people who opt for a life in the West and will thereby be lost forever to Burmese society. In any case, nothing will change in Burma's situation if it is only the effects of the disaster that are treated and not the root causes.

There are believed to be up to two million illegal Burmese immigrants in Thailand. Without any valid papers and work permits, they might at any minute be deported back to Burma if they cannot raise sufficient funds to bribe the officials. Furthermore, since they have no rights, they are at the mercy of their Thai employers, and are often very badly paid or not even paid at all. Prostitution and sexual diseases like HIV/Aids are on the increase among the migrants, and although the Thai government recently introduced a programme of registration to enable them to work legally, many of them cannot afford the $100 (£50) fee.

None of the neighbouring countries that have accepted the Burmese have granted them official refugee status. They have a very restrictive immigration policy and discriminative laws in the hope that they can get rid of the refugees as quickly as possible and not jeopardize relations with the Burmese junta. In some Thai provinces, for instance, migrants were not allowed to use mobile phones, drive motorcycles or cars and go out at night for reasons of national security.

Below: Burmese refugees behind bars, Mae Sot, Thailand

Opposite: Mae La camp, just 30 kilometres from the border towns of Mae Sot and Myawaddy

Kayan Women ကယန်းအမျိုးသမီး

The villages of the ethnic groups are a major tourist attraction in Thailand. Many of them come from Burma and have left their homes because of the civil war, and one of these peoples is the Kayan (also known as Padaung), who are a branch of the Karen. There are various subdivisions of the Kayan that can be distinguished mainly by their costumes and decorations. Kayan women are world-famous for their long necks, around which they wear brass rings. This decoration is exclusive to females, and even little girls get their first rings at the age of four, which are wound around the neck in a spiral. The number of rings is increased every year so that the shoulders are weighed down, compressing the rib cage and thus creating the illusion of an extended neck. The final weight of these rings can be anything up to 10 kg (22 lb).

There are different stories surrounding this striking decoration. According to one legend, the Kayan are descended from a birdlike angel and a dragon mother. Kayan women are therefore said to be trying to imitate the long necks of their remote ancestor. It is also suggested that in former times the rings were meant to distinguish the Kayan from other nations. Other explanations suggest that the rings are used to stop women from marrying into other ethnic peoples or may even offer protection against tiger bites. Not all the Kayan people have taken this necklace into their culture; some simply wear metal rings around their legs or arms. For some time now, there has been opposition to this custom of wearing rings, not only because it is felt to be out of keeping with modern times, but because it is a heavy burden for the girls and women who have to wear them. In Burma itself, the Kayan live near Loikaw, in Karenni State, which was always their traditional home, although many have now fled because of the war between the KNPP and the *Tatmadaw*. The Kayan are therefore split between Burma and Thailand, but travellers are unable to visit those who are left in the Loikaw area because most of the time the state is barred to foreigners.

In Thailand, on the other hand, the refugee villages are open to those willing to pay the entrance fee. Visitors watch the women in a kind of human zoo as they go about their daily work, sell their textiles and other souvenirs, or allow them to take their photographs. Although this earns the Kayan a modest income, the bulk of the money goes to Thai businessmen. In order to remain a tourist attraction and thus to be able to feed their families, there are still plenty of girls willing to wear the heavy rings and thus artificially to prolong the life of this dubious tradition.

From an early age, Kayan women wear brass rings to make their necks look longer

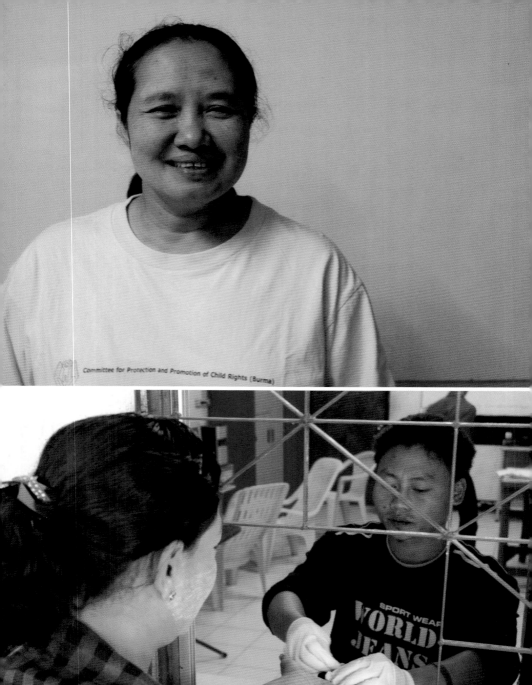
Committee for Protection and Promotion of Child Rights (Burma)

The Mae Tao Clinic မယ်တော်ဆေးခန်း

The Mae Tao Clinic in Mae Sot on the Thai/Burmese border was founded in 1989 by Dr Cynthia Maung. The atrocities committed by the Burmese Army in the aftermath of the mass uprising in 1988 forced her to flee, along with thousands of her compatriots, to neighbouring Thailand. Initially, her intention was to give medical aid to the refugee activists, but very soon her clinic was also serving Internally Displaced Persons in Burma as well as Burmese migrants seeking work in Thailand.

In addition to providing healthcare, the clinic offers training places for nurses and auxiliary workers, and gives medical advice to mothers and children. A school for 400 migrant children and a centre for victims of sexual abuse and domestic violence were also set up. Over the years, the different sections of the clinic have constantly expanded with the aid of foreign non-governmental organizations and the Thai health service. There are now wards and departments for first aid, general practice, obstetrics, eye diseases, trauma, prostheses for the many victims of landmines, and a blood bank. Of the 60,000–80,000 patients treated every year, many cross the border illegally from Burma, after perilous journeys through the jungle lasting several days, to get to the only place that can offer them medical aid. In 2000 the World Health Organization ranked Burma's health service as the second worst in the world, and in any case treatment is only available in the large towns. Rural regions, especially close to the borders, receive virtually no healthcare at all.

Malaria, a particularly resistant form of which is rampant along the border between Burma and Thailand, is infecting more and more of the population, but also massively on the increase are malnutrition – especially among children – and HIV/Aids. Very serious cases cannot be treated in the Mae Tao Clinic itself and have to be referred to Thai hospitals. The large but overcrowded wards in the clinic have only the simplest

Opposite: (above) Dr Cynthia Maung; (below) laboratory at the Mae Tao Clinic, Mae Sot, Thailand

Right: newborn twins, Mae Tao Clinic

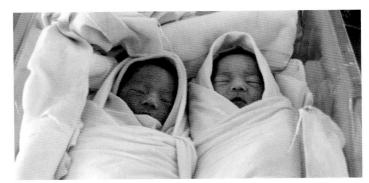

equipment, and most of the patients lie on thin mattresses or simple wooden beds. Members of the family help to look after them. For her selfless work and unceasing devotion to all the people of Burma, Dr Cynthia has been given many human rights awards, and has also been proposed for the Nobel Peace Prize. She herself is extraordinarily modest about her achievements and accepts the interest in her as a necessary evil that enables her to help the people of her country and to draw the world's attention to their catastrophic plight.

Backpacker Medics

In 1998 Dr Cynthia Maung set up the Backpack Health Worker Team (BPHWT), with medics active in the regions of the Mon, Karen and Karenni. Today there are seventy-six teams with over 300 health workers from all ethnic groups in Burma bringing medical care to the IDPs and people in the 'Black Zones' of the country, where absolutely no healthcare system exists. Since 2006 these have also been joined by BPHWTs in the Shan and Lahu regions, which are estimated to be treating around 140,000 patients a year.

These health workers are given six months' training in Thailand – some of them at the Mae Tao Clinic – and are then sent back to their village communities in Burma. There they live with the IDPs, and move with them from place to place when they come under attack from the SPDC. A team consists of three to five workers and looks after some 2,000 people.

There are three main programmes that the backpackers offer:
1. Basic medical treatment
2. Health education and prevention of disease within the community
3. Family planning and welfare for mothers and children

They also collect data, using photos and video documentation to record the health situation in the crisis regions. Workshops and training courses are held on the spot when needed because the main aim of the backpackers is to help people to help themselves.

In order to bring treatment to the IDPs, the BPHWTs put themselves in real danger. They may travel on foot for days through the jungle, carrying bamboo baskets full of medicines and materials on their backs. When they pass through SPDC areas, they have to go by night without any form of lighting, because if they are caught they will be killed. They are unarmed, and the only protection they get is from local freedom fighters such as the KNLA and the SSA-S. Despite all their precautions, many of them have sacrificed their lives, either shot by the *Tatmadaw* or blown up by landmines. The latter are widespread throughout the border regions, and often the backpackers have to carry out emergency amputations with the most basic equipment, or take the injured on bamboo stretchers across the border to clinics in Thailand.

Opposite: (above) backpacker medic in the field; (below) polio sufferer, Mae Tao Clinic

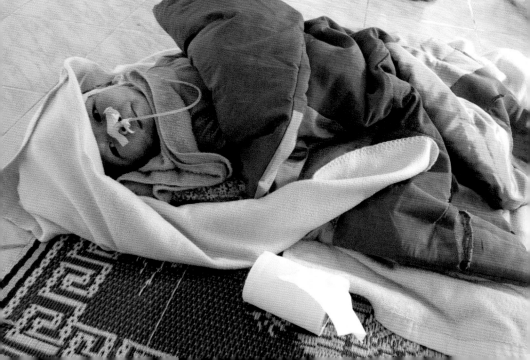

Assistance Association for Political Prisoners
အကျဉ်းသားများ ကူညီစောင့်ရှောက်ရေး အဖွဲ့

The life of a political activist in Burma is one of extreme danger, and so many go underground. There are almost 2,000 political prisoners languishing in the grim depths of Burmese prisons or slaving away in forced labour camps, and over 120 have died behind bars in recent times.

In 1999 a group of former political prisoners and activists came together in the Thai border town of Mae Sot, with the aim of helping their colleagues who were still in prison. The Assistance Association for Political Prisoners (Burma) – AAPP(b) – was officially established in March 2000. Today the association runs a little museum in Mae Sot, which gives a very clear image of conditions for political prisoners in Burma. Former detainees guide visitors round the exhibition room and describe their own experiences.

In an interview of February 2008, Nay Rein Kyaw recalls his own interrogation: 'Upon arrival at the interrogation center I was separated from my friends and sent to a dimly lit dirty room where I was handcuffed and ordered to stand in front of a table. The MI asked me many questions. When they were not satisfied with my answers, they would force me to continuously squat and stand. When I tried to stop, they kicked and punched me many times and hit my knees with a bamboo rod. When I fell down on to the concrete floor, they grabbed me by the arm and pulled me upright. For another type of torture, I was put on a hollow chair and electric wires were attached to my arm so that they could give me electric shocks. I had no chance to sleep or rest for nearly three days and during this time I was given no water or food. I was so thirsty that I asked to go to the toilet hoping that I could take some water from there. However the guards watched me the

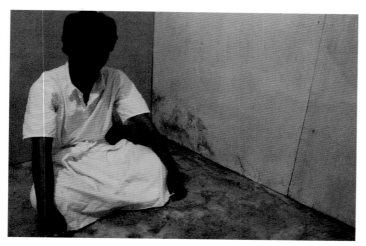

Re-enactment of a Burmese prisoner in the *pohsan* position, which is used as a form of torture

Insein prison, near Rangoon. Conditions in Burma's prisons are appalling, and political prisoners receive special treatment. Soon after they have been arrested, they are taken to the notorious interrogation centres and brutally tortured. Frequently they are beaten unconscious during the hearings, or made to stand or squat for several hours in unnatural positions, and women are often raped.

entire time and when I attempted to drink some water from the pot by the toilet they hit me. I was also kept blindfolded for the entire two weeks that I was at the interrogation centre.'

They are generally allowed no legal representation, and confessions are not infrequently extorted from them before they are thrown into jail. But this does not mark the end of the ordeal. The cells are hopelessly overcrowded, and inmates have to sleep on the cold stone floor and share a bucket for a lavatory. It is the perfect breeding ground for bacteria and disease. Just once a month, or at best once a week, they are given a few pails of water to shower with. Food and fresh drinking water are kept to a minimum. Everyday life comprises torture, abuse, beatings, deprivation of food, drink and sleep, and in some cases debilitating solitary confinement. The aim of prison life is to break the will of the political activist by psychological and physical torture. Family visits are allowed for fifteen minutes every fortnight, and these bring welcome relief because family members are the only chance the prisoners have of receiving medication, clothing or food.

The AAPP(b) compile reports about current political prisoners, their state of health and their location. They collect photographs as well as eyewitness accounts, and try to give direct support to the inmates with medicines and food. Frequently they are forced to do their work underground.

Once prisoners have been released, the organization continues to take care of them, because they are still likely to be persecuted by the authorities and prevented from getting work owing to their political record. The AAPP(b) have published several books describing the torture and appalling conditions in Burma's prisons, and they have also produced some books of poetry.

Glossary

anda the bell- or dome-shaped upper part of a stupa

Bamar Burmese ethnic group

cheroot Burmese cigar containing tobacco and herbs, wrapped in a leaf

chinlon ball game in which players must pass the ball without dropping it on the floor or using their hands

chinthe mythical lion-like creature, often guarding pagoda entrances

deva (Sanskrit) 'beaming', divine creatures

duwa Kachin prince

dvarapala (Sanskrit) guardian figure, traditionally placed outside Buddhist temples

haw Shan word for 'palace'

hti decorated umbrella-like feature at the tip of a stupa

Jataka (Sanskrit) birth stories of the Buddha

longyi unisex sarong-like garment

mahadevi (Sanskrit) 'great goddess', official title for the Shan queen

Manau Kachin festival

Manuthiha mythical creatures with one head and two bodies

mara (Sanskrit) standing for death and disaster, this Satan-like figure tries to tempt the Buddha

naga (Sanskrit) mythical snake, guardian of the life energy

nat spirit being that has the power to either protect or punish people

ogre mythical monster figure

Padaung another word for the Kayan ethnic group

pahto Burmese word for temple with a hollow interior

Pali ancient language in which the Buddhist scriptures were written

pohsan form of torture by which political prisoners are forced to squat in unnatural positions for hours

pwe cultural festival

Sanskrit ancient Indo-European language of India, from which many Burmese words derive

sao princely Shan title

saopha (or *sawbwa* in Burmese) Shan word for their prince

sayadaw 'master teacher', the title for a highly honoured Buddhist monk

shikhara (Sanskrit) top of a stupa in which the rising tower has a corncob-like appearance

stupa (Sanskrit) meaning 'grave mound', place in a pagoda where Buddha relics were kept and where it is forbidden to enter

Suvarnabhumi (Sanskrit) 'Golden Land', synonym for the land of the Mon in ancient times

Tatmadaw Burmese Army

thakin a word meaning 'master', which was used during the Burmese national movement

thakinma female version of *thakin*

thanakha a paste made from ground wood, used as sunblock and make-up

Tipitaka the sacred canon of Theravada Buddhism, written in Pali

trishaw Burmese bicycle rickshaw

yaba infamous drug, a derivative of synthetic amphetamines

Websites

News from Burma:
Burma Digest: burmadigest.info
Burma Issues: burmaissues.org
Burma Library: burmalibrary.org
Democratic Voice of Burma: dvb.no
The Irrawaddy: irrawaddy.org
Mizzima: mizzima.com
Shan Herald Agency for News: shanland.org

Burma Groups:
Burma Aktion (GER): burmaaktion.de
Burma Bureau (GER): burmabureaugermany.com

Burma Campaign (UK): burmacampaign.org.uk
Burma Centrum Nederland (NL): burmacentrum.nl
Burma.Initiative (GER): asienhaus.de/burma
US Campaign for Burma (USA): http://uscampaignforburma.org/

Aid Organizations:
Assistance Association for Political Prisoners (Burma): aappb.org
Help without Frontiers: helfenohnegrenzen.org
Mae Tao Clinic: maetaoclinic.org

Shan Women's Action Network: shanwomen.org
UNHCR: unhcr.org

Other Websites:
Aung San Suu Kyi: dassk.org
Burma Art Shop: burmaart.de
Free Burma Rangers: freeburmarangers.org
Nicholas Ganz: keinom.com
Human Rights Watch: hrw.org
International Labour Organization: ilo.org
Karen Human Rights Group: khrg.org

The Regime's Official Website:
myanmar.com

Further Reading

Aung San Suu Kyi, *Freedom from Fear*, London: Penguin, 1995

Aung San Suu Kyi, *Letters from Burma*, London: Penguin, 1997

Aung San Suu Kyi, *The Voice of Hope*, London: Penguin, 1997

Dean Chapman, *Karenni: Guerrilla in Burma*, Stockport: Dewi Lewis Publishing, 1998

Russ Christensen & Sann Kyaw, *The Pa-O: Rebels and Refugees*, Chiang Mai: Silkworm Books, 2006

Alan Clements & Leslie Kean, *Burma's Revolution of the Spirit: The Struggle for Democratic Freedom and Dignity*, Bangkok: White Orchid Press, 1995

Maurice Collis, *Lords of the Sunset: A Tour in the Shan States*, Bangkok: Ava House, 1996 (first published by Faber & Faber, London, 1938)

Jan Donkers & Minka Nijhuis, *Burma Behind the Mask*, Amsterdam: Burma Centrum Nederland, 1996

Patricia W. Elliott, *The White Umbrella: A Woman's Struggle for Freedom in Burma*, second edition, Bangkok: Friends Books, 2006

Bertil Lintner, *Outrage: Burma's Struggle for Democracy*, London: White Lotus, 1990

Bertil Lintner, *Land of Jade: A Journey Through Insurgent Burma*, Bangkok: White Orchid Press, 1990

Bertil Lintner, *The Kachin: Lords of Burma's Northern Frontier*, Chiang Mai: Asia Film House, 1997

Bertil Lintner, *Burma in Revolt: Opium and Insurgency since 1948*, Chiang Mai: Silkworm Books, 1999

Andrew Marshall, *The Trouser People: A Quest for the Victorian Footballer Who Made Burma Play the Empire's Game*, London: Penguin Books, 2003

Inge Sargent, *Twilight over Burma: My Life as a Shan Princess*, Chiang Mai: Silkworm Books, 1994

J.D. Saul, *The Naga of Burma: Their Festivals, Customs, and Way of Life*, Bangkok: Orchid Press, 2005

J. George Scott, *Burma: A Handbook of Practical Information*, Bangkok: Orchid Press, 1999 (first published in 1906)

Shway Yoe (J. George Scott), *The Burman: His Life and Notions*, New York: Norton Library, 1963 (first published in 1882)

Martin Smith, *Burma: Insurgency and the Politics of Ethnicity*, London, New York & Bangkok: Zed Books Ltd / White Lotus Co., 1999

Phil Thornton, *Restless Souls: Rebels, Refugees, Medics and Misfits on the Thai-Burma Border*, Bangkok: Asia Books, 2006

Acknowledgments

This book is dedicated to all the people of Burma. May their dreams of freedom and self-determination come true. This book would never have been possible without the generous support and trust of so many people, some of whom have to remain anonymous for their own safety.

In Germany we would like to thank Aung Than Oo (Sonny) and Nwe Aung in particular, who both gave us a fantastic opportunity to delve deeper into the subject. Meetings with you have always been a great joy! Thanks also to Swe Myint Swe for the great food in the Mandalay restaurant in Cologne. Ulrike Bey from the Burma.Initiative in Essen has also given us tremendous support.

Many thanks also go to Karl Förster for sharing his time and thoughts with us, helping us with our cross-border human-aid and for his great personal work for the people in Burma.

We also thank the SSA-S of Loi Taileng for being so hospitable during our stays, especially Yawd Muang who gave us a helping hand as a translator and guide. Thanks also to Ma Ha Ngern, who was very helpful with the translation of our interviews. We also owe deep thanks to all the refugees, students and soldiers in Loi Taileng who were willing to tell their stories and let us into their lives. We hope your dreams for your future come true.

Many people in the Mae Hongson area have helped us with our work. Thanks to Hkun Okker and especially Hkun Tetlu and all the staff from the PPLO office, who introduced us to people in this area.

In Mae Sot we are very grateful for the support of Dr Kyaw Nyunt, who was always very helpful with all our queries. Thanks also go to Mahn Mahn, Dr Htawsoe from the BPHWT and to Dr Cynthia Maung for giving up precious time to answer our questions.

We also thank all the civilian journalists who showed such courage in taking photos of the 2007 Saffron Revolution.

We have a great deal of respect for all the people we have met in Burma and in the border regions. So many of you will remain unnamed here but thank you for sharing your time with us and for giving us the opportunity to listen to your stories.

We also thank everyone at Thames & Hudson for making this project possible.

Our deepest thanks also go to our families, our parents Ingeborg and Bojan Jotow and Corina and Hartmut Ganz, our brothers Niki Jotow and his family and Maurice and René Ganz, for their unswerving support and understanding.

Thanks to Ingo Ahlborn for his creative input, Julie Büchel for the difficulties she faced as security back-up, Ayscha Lucas for sharing her feelings and thoughts during our work on this book, Nele Engelhardt and Sophie Köhler for supporting us in many ways, and last but not least Anne Traphan and Viviane Radtke for being the godmothers of this book.

About the Authors

Geographer Elena Jotow and photographer Nicholas Ganz are freelance authors based in Essen, Germany. They have worked and travelled extensively in Burma and founded the Burma Aktion group to support Burmese refugees and organizations along the border. Ganz's previous books include *Graffiti World* (2004) and *Graffiti Woman* (2006).

Index